Human Resource Management

In-Basket Exercises for School Administrators

Jerry R. Baker
Madeleine S. Doran

A SCARECROWEDUCATION BOOK

The Scarecrow Press, Inc.
Lanham, Maryland, and Oxford
2002

MT

Published in the United States of America
by ScarecrowEducation
An imprint of The Rowman & Littlefield Publishing Group, Inc.
4501 Forbes Boulevard, Suite 200, Lanham, Maryland 20706
www.scaroweducation.com

PO Box 317
Oxford
OX2 9RU, UK

British Library Cataloguing in Publication Information Available

Library of Congress Cataloging-in-Publication Data

Baker, Jerry R., 1938–
  Human resource management : in-basket exercises for school administrators /
Jerry R. Baker, Madeleine S. Doran.
     p. cm.
"A ScarecrowEducation book."
Includes bibliographical references and index.
  ISBN 0-8108-4518-0 (pbk. : alk. paper)
  1. School personnel management—Problems, exercises, etc. 2. School
administrators—Training of—Problems, exercises, etc. I. Doran, Madeleine S.,
1943– II. Title.
  LB2831.5 .B35 2002
  371.2'01—dc21   2002009745

♾™ The paper used in this publication meets the minimum requirements of
American National Standard for Information Sciences—Permanence of
Paper for Printed Library Materials, ANSI/NISO Z39.48-1992.
Manufactured in the United States of America.

4/27/04

Contents

PREFACE

This publication is not a traditional textbook dealing with human resource management. Rather, it is a tool for training and assessing school administrators using in-basket exercises based on issues and situations encountered in today's workplace. Working through the in-basket exercises included in this publication will give students an opportunity to apply their knowledge and skills to situations they are very likely to face on the job.

The authors envision this publication being used primarily in two ways:

1. Graduate courses in human resource management offered by Colleges of Education as part of their preparation program in School Administration and

2. School district initiated professional development programs designed for principals and assistant principals (as well as those planning to assume administrative roles in the future.)

It has long been recognized that principals in small school districts must be well trained in the various functions of school administration. In small school districts, central office specialists are simply not available to assist the building principal. Today, because of downsizing of the central office staff in many medium and large-sized districts, the principal must assume many of the responsibilities once the domain of the central office. Similarly, initiatives designed to decentralize the administration of school districts and other school-based decision making efforts, contribute significantly to the increase in the level of responsibility of the principal. Today more than ever before, the principal must be able to address human resource management issues and problems.

Many private sector organizations and a few school districts design professional development programs for their future managers that include multiple internship opportunities. In some school districts individuals preparing for a principalship are asked to serve a brief internship in the following departments: a) Curriculum and Instruction, b) Human Resources, and c) Business and Finance. This is excellent preparation for the principalship. Unfortunately, in education, because of the added expense, this practice is not widespread.

Most school districts do not have the financial resources to place aspiring school administrators in internships as part of their preparation. The authors believe that this publication can provide a substitute for the internship experience in human resource management due to its high workplace realism.

The authors have relied on a combined 35 years of school human resource management experience to provide perspective to the complexity and diversity of human resource issues. It is critical that school administrators have an understanding of human resource management. If not handled appropriately, such issues create negative publicity and can result in costly litigation.

Each of the experiential exercises included in this publication is based on realistic situations similar to those the authors have experienced and reflect the array of issues, opportunities and problems that confront the school administrator.

Chapters 1, 2 and 3 include:

- A brief history of assessment centers;
- An abbreviated review of research validating the use of in-basket exercises for training and assessment;
- A synopsis of recognized adult learning theories;
- Suggestions to the instructor regarding the use of the exercises; and
- A description of a fictitious school district that provides the "setting" for the in-basket exercises.

Chapter 4 includes:

- Suggestions to the student regarding the completion of the in-basket exercises; and
- One hundred twenty in-basket exercises grouped into 12 categories that comprise the major components of human resource management.

With this publication, the authors have attempted to provide a resource for instructors and students that is based on real-life problems and issues in human resource management.

The authors welcome comments and/or suggestions and can be reached at their respective universities.

ACKNOWLEDGMENTS

The authors would like to take this opportunity to thank our colleagues for their help, encouragement and support during the writing of this book. In addition, we would like to acknowledge the graduate students who, during field-testing of the in-basket exercises, made invaluable suggestions and provided constructive criticism.

The authors are also indebted to Susan J. Baker who made an extensive contribution to the preparation of the manuscript. Finally, the authors would like to express their appreciation to the School District of Lee County for permitting the authors to reprint selected sections of their collective bargaining agreements.

CHAPTER 1

Introduction

Purpose of the Publication

A school district's most significant asset is its people. Employee compensation represents 70–80% of the typical district's annual operating budget. Therefore, it is critical that educational leaders be well versed in human resource management (HRM). Ivancevich (1998, p. 5) defines HRM as follows: "Human resource management is the function performed in organizations that facilitates the most effective use of people (employees) to achieve organizational and individual goals." Major components of a HRM system include employee recruitment, selection, contract administration, performance appraisal, compensation, collective bargaining, employee relations, including investigations and discipline, and employee training and development.

The contributions HRM make to an organization are significant. Ivancevich cites the following:

- Helping the organization reach its goals
- Employing the skills and abilities of the work-force efficiently
- Providing the organization with well trained and well motivated employees
- Increasing to the fullest the employee's job satisfaction and self actualization
- Developing and maintaining a quality of work life that makes employment in the organization desirable
- Communicating HRM policies to all employees
- Helping to maintain ethical policies and socially responsible behavior
- Managing change to the mutual advantage of individuals, groups, the enterprise, and the public. (p. 9)

The human resources (people) of a school district are vitally important. Proper management of these resources is essential as school districts strive to become more effective and efficient.

1

The purpose of this publication is to provide a training and assessment resource for current and aspiring school administrators based on real-world human resource management problems and issues. To accomplish this, the authors have drawn on some of the methodology of assessment centers and in-baskets exercises.

Concept and Evolution of Assessment Centers

The origin of the modern-day assessment center had its roots in Germany in the 1930s. Germany was the first to use situational tests of leadership as a basis for selection. Although somewhat crude, the process required candidates to take part in leadership exercises and have their behavior critiqued by trained observers (Wendel and Joekel, 1991).

Early in WWII, the British became disenchanted with drafting graduates of the elite schools with officer training programs and adapted a program similar to the one used in Germany. Aware of Germany's shortcomings, however, the British expanded the assessment exercises to include a number of group tasks, including problem solving and leaderless groups. After WWII, the British Civil Service Selection Board, having responsibility for selecting administrators for civil service positions, developed a multi-assessment process. This transition to a civilian organization paved the way for assessment centers in the private sector (Wendel and Joekel, 1991).

Initial use of the assessment center model in the United States occurred early in WWII as a result of a serious personnel problem encountered by General "Wild Bill" Donovan, head of the Office of Strategic Services (OSS), predecessor of the CIA. A large number of spies and secret agents were needed to serve behind enemy lines. Given the challenging and clandestine nature of their activities, it became necessary to develop a battery of tests to determine candidates' fitness for duty and their likelihood of success and a safe return. The tests included leaderless group activities and situational exercises designed to measure leadership ability, ingenuity and stress tolerance (Wendel and Joekel, 1991).

American Telephone and Telegraph's Management Progress Study (MPS) is one of the most significant research studies designed to determine the predictability of assessment center results to improve the recruiting and training of managers. The participants were processed through AT&T's center and evaluated for their likelihood of being promoted to a management position within 10 years at AT&T. The results were sealed and neither the participants nor their supervisors were aware of the assessment results. Within 8 years, 42% of the participants predicted to be promoted held management positions while only 7% of those not rated as "promotable" had been promoted. As a result, the study revealed that multiple assessment techniques were successful in predicting managerial success (Wendel and Joekel, 1991).

Today assessment centers operate in 70% of organizations in the United Kingdom and more than 2,000 companies in the United States (Griffiths and Goodge, 1994). Fueling the widespread acceptance of the assessment center is the high cost of mistakes in personnel selection as well as the favorable responses from the court system where they are accepted as job-related and unbiased. Wendel and Joekel (1991) draw an analogy between the criteria used to select the players for a National Basketball Association franchise and those used to select potential school administrators. They describe the assessment center as a method "which is designed to assess specific job-related skills and behaviors under simulated 'game conditions'" (p. 8).

The traditional assessment center model includes the following elements (Taylor, 1990):

- *Job Analysis*: A review of the position description, interviews with incumbents and a collection of work samples are used to create the skills and characteristics required.
- *Exercise Development*: Using the job analysis data, a number of exercises are created to give the candidate an opportunity to demonstrate his/her abilities.
- *Candidate Orientation*: An orientation to the process satisfies the candidate's "need to know," thereby reducing anxiety and improving chances for success.
- *Evaluator Training*: To assess results in a standardized manner, it is critical that the evaluators be trained.
- *Candidate Evaluation*: Each candidate's evaluation is discussed and the ratings are determined independently or by consensus.

Taylor (1990) cites four governmental entities—Loveland, Colorado, Richmond, Virginia, San Diego County, California, and Gillette, Wyoming—that use assessment centers to select employees for management and supervisory positions, for promotional purposes and as a tool for training and development. Diane McCoy, personnel director in Loveland, says "without a doubt, assessment centers favorably influence decisions" (p. 3). In a recent hiring situation, if only the traditional interview had been used, a different candidate would have been selected for the position. According to McCoy, the incumbent has proved to be an

3

excellent choice, but would not have been selected without the assessment center (Taylor, 1990).

The most widely used assessment center in education is the National Association of Secondary School Administrators (NASSP) Assessment Center Project for the selection of school principals. A number of universities also are affiliated with the NASSP Assessment Center Project and train assessors to administer centers in their own school districts as well as use it for their own administrator preparation programs.

The Frontier Central Schools (K–12) in Hamburg, New York, exercised an alternative to the traditional search and interview process when faced with the task of hiring a new superintendent. The school board was not confident that interviews alone would ensure it would find a superintendent who met the community's specific needs. An assessment process was designed that included a series of in-basket items, which required applicants to set priorities and provide a rationale for their decisions. Other exercises involved role-playing or simulation. Chuck Little, selected as school superintendent, said that the in-basket exercise allowed the candidate to be more creative and thoughtful while the role-playing exercise required applicants to "think quickly on their feet" (Collins, 1999, p. 36).

The In-Basket Exercise

The in-basket model was selected for use in this publication because of its advantages in both training and assessment. The paragraphs that follow summarize the nature of in-basket exercises as well as selected research findings associated with their use.

Hakstian and Scratchley (1997) identified the in-basket exercise as a major component in assessment centers for either training and development or management selection decisions. An in-basket exercise is a simulation using materials that would typically appear in the in-basket of a hypothetical manager. These materials may be in the form of telephone messages, letters, memos or reports and each requires interpretation and reaction by the participant. "A wide variety of job content can be represented in this way and the participant's responses are either subjectively rated or empirically scored in a way that reflects the individual's level of performance" (Schippmann, 1990, p. 837). "The major appeal of the in-basket exercise in management assessment is its high face validity" (Hakstian and Scratchley, 1997, p. 608). There is empirical evidence that the in-basket has solid criterion-related validity (Kellesman,

Lopez and Lopez, 1982; Schippmann, Prien and Katz, 1990; Hakstian and Harlos, 1993).

"The key to the in-basket's effectiveness as a training device is that it needs to be rooted in real-life situations" (Mallick and Stumpf, 1998, p. 40). Clearly, the high workplace realism provided by means of the in-basket makes it ideal for training purposes. Gill (1979) notes that in-baskets are particularly helpful for assessing recall, identifying issues and promoting critical and analytical thinking, including the establishment of priorities. As participants take on the role of the hypothetical manager, it requires them to "appreciate subtleties and technical niceties that always complicate any management problem" (Lopez, 1966, p. 68). The in-basket exercises allow for the "differentiation between issues of content and process but permit one to examine both" (Dukerich and Milliken, 1990, p. 407).

In-basket exercises have been used extensively in assessment centers. Gill (1979) and Bender (1973) found them to be the most common method to assess managerial potential in the United States. Gill (1979) finds they are generally perceived to be high in face validity because they require participants to become involved in an important aspect of managerial behavior. Their widespread use by companies such as IBM and the Bell System is further testimony to their face validity (Dukerich, 1990). Schippmann (1990) cites favorable reports of their use as an assessment device from Bentz's 1968 work at Sears and the Bray and Grant (1966) studies at AT&T.

While in-baskets were traditionally designed for the selection of employees with strong potential for management roles, more recently they have been extended to career development and the selection of people to fit new work designs, such as self-managing teams (Englebreacht and Fischer, 1995). Recent research suggests that assessment centers contribute to promotability when participants are willing to address and work on their developmental needs (Jones and Whitmore, 1995).

The in-basket has received favorable reports from Lopez's 1966 work with Boeing, Montgomery Ward and the New York Port Authority (Schippmann, 1990). "When used for developmental purposes, assessment centers can provide employees with the support and direction they need for career development" (Cummings and Worley, 1993, p. 411).

Montuori and Kimmel (1994) investigated the feasibility of teaching conceptual complexity to adults using in-basket simulation. Conceptual complexity/simplicity refers to the degree to which an individual both discriminates among and integrates multidimensional information. "The continuum runs from one–dimensional information processing and ensuing decision making (conceptual simplicity), on the extreme low end of the conceptual scale, to multidimensional information processing and resulting decision-making (conceptual complexity) on the high end of the scale" (p. 4). The authors concluded that the "overall training effect was significant, confirming the research hypothesis that conceptual complexity can be improved through explicit training" (p. 3).

The Adult Learner

Malcom Knowles is credited with bringing the theory that distinguishes between the teaching of children and the teaching of adults, otherwise known as andragogy, to the United States. It is based on the following assumptions (Knowles, Holton, Swanson, 1998, p. 64):

- *The need to know*: Adults need to know why they need to learn something.
- *The learner's self-concept*: Adults maintain the concept of responsibility for their own decisions and lives.
- *The role of the learners' experiences*: Adults enter educational environment with life experiences.
- *Readiness to learn*: Adults have a readiness to learn those things they need to know in order to cope effectively with real-life situations.
- *Orientation to learning*: Adults are life-centered in their orientation to learning.
- *Motivation*: Adults are more responsive to internal motivators.

Items 3 and 5 are closely related in that current experience is a major factor in motivating adults to learn. "Adults generally prefer a problem solving orientation to learning rather than subject-centered learning. Furthermore, they learn best when new information is presented in real-life context" (Knowles, Holton, Swanson, 1998, p. 146).

Learning may be categorized as passive or experiential, although the categories are not discrete. Passive learning occurs when the instructor uses lecture, discussion, individual exercises, reading, case analysis and individual assignments. Experiential learning activities include role-playing, management games, in-baskets and sensitivity training (Mailick, 1998). The major difference between the two is that in passive education the performance of one participant does not have an impact on another. A critic of the traditional passive academic training writes, "The case

6

method, lectures, discussions and theories of various kinds have been around for some time. They are helpful exercises for mind stretching. But how much of that instruction ever finds its way back to the office" (Livingston, 1983, p. 15). Passive learning may increase cognitive knowledge. It may even change attitudes. The real test of learning, however, is whether there is a change in behavior—the translation of knowledge into action.

Mailick (1998) maintains, "experiential learning is more effective than passive learning for integrating new learning with experience" (p. 24). Experiential learning requires the exploring and testing of cause and effect and includes analysis and the evaluation and selection of alternative courses of action. Researchers also have focused on experiential learning as a means to enhance transfer of learning into performance (Holton, Bates, Seyler and Carvalho, 1997).

David Kolb (1984), a leading advocate of experiential learning, based his model on Kurt Lewin's problem-solving model of action research. He categorizes learning into four processes: concrete experience; reflective observation; abstract conceptualization; and active experimentation. Kolb (1984) defines learning as "The process whereby knowledge is created through transformation of experience" (p. 38). The interrelationship between content and experience serves to transform each, and it is up to the instructor to facilitate the generation of new ideas and transform the old ideas that inhibit new learning. The in-basket model most closely matches Kolb's concrete experience cycle of learning. When faced with "real world" human resource issues that confront school administrators, students likely will identify the behaviors that lead to the most satisfying results.

There is no question that training and development efforts must include specialized competencies. There is a growing need, however, to focus on the development of integrative learning. Integrative learning is more concerned with the process of executive problem solving and the ability to discern which competence to apply in a given situation (Kola, Lublin, Stuart, Spoth, Baker, 1994). A major advantage of the in-basket exercise is that it allows for the differentiation between issues of content and process but permits the learner to examine both (Dukerich and Milliken, 1990). One of the methods used to facilitate integrative learning is dialogue, an open communication process where ideas and feelings are shared in a spirit of cooperation and inquiry. The cooperative spirit must not be construed to mean that differences of opinion should not be openly expressed. Integrative learning thrives when there is conflict and differences in points of view and those differences are examined constructively. This process development is strengthened by the group approach to solving the in-basket problems and provides the tools for students to cope with similar issues when they occur in the workplace.

In summary, issues relating to human resource management are among the most challenging facing school principals and other administrators. The principal's ability to deal with these issues affects faculty and staff morale and, ultimately, student achievement. The in-basket exercises in this publication are ideal for training because of their high workplace realism. The exercises provide for the integration of knowledge and experience and provide skill development in both process and content, which leads to a higher degree of transfer to the workplace. The in-basket exercises meet the characteristics of adult learning theory. While they most closely match Kolb's (1984) concrete experience learning process, a creative instructor will diversify instructional methods to incorporate reflective observation, abstract conceptualization and active experimenta-tion.

CHAPTER 2

Using This Publication

The diversity of the in-basket exercises in this publication reflects the complexity and ambiguity of human resources situations that face the school professional. Each situation has been carefully considered and selected for its realism and relevance to the educational setting. Although presented entirely in written form via letter, note, memorandum or e-mail, in the real world many of the situations occur face-to-face, at meetings or in other situations.

The in-basket exercises may be used for training and/or assessment. They may be used by school districts as a tool for screening and selecting applicants for positions or in career development programs for diagnosing developmental needs of current and aspiring school administrators.

The in-basket exercises may also be used in an instructional setting or for training. The exercises provide a rich source of material for students' introspection, analysis, discussion, debate and reflection. When used as a group exercise, conflict and debate will energize the problem-solving process. Many of the exercises offer opportunities for students to research current topics and practices in the field in order to prepare an acceptable response. A list of suggested readings follows each category and provides background information for use in working through the exercises. The instructor may use the exercises as follows:

	TRAINING	ASSESSMENT
Individual Student	In-class activity/ assignment Take-home assignment	In-class activity/ assignment (timed) Take-home assignment (untimed)
Small Groups	Discussion, Analysis and Presentation	Project/Presentation
Large Groups	Discussion and Analysis	In-class (timed) Take-home exam (untimed)

Suggestions for the Instructor Using This Publication

When used in a graduate course in human resource management, this publication can be used as a supplement to a traditional textbook or as the only publication required of all students. During field-testing, this publication was the only publication required of all students. However, students were informed that they would need to seek out information from other sources in order to address the issues presented in the in-basket exercises. Students were asked to consider the following options:

    A. Use the resources available at the university library.
    B. Search the Internet for necessary background information.
    C. Purchase a traditional human resources management text.
    D. Discuss exercises with practicing professionals in the field.
    E. A combination of the above.

A majority of students chose a combination of options A and B.

In addition to the students' efforts to seek out the information (literature) needed to respond to the in-basket exercises, the instructor may provide information in several ways. During field-testing, the authors typically: 1) introduced each category of in-basket exercises, 2) provided handouts, and/or 3) suggested specific readings associated with the exercises under consideration. In addition, the authors provided information while critiquing students' responses during class discussions. Information was also provided, by way of a summary, before moving on to the next category of in-basket exercises.

It should be noted that the in-basket exercises included in this publication take place in the Melita Public Schools. In this fictitious school district CJ Castle, Director of Human Resources, is the central figure. Students working through the in-basket exercises are asked to assume the role of CJ Castle. A description of the Melita Public Schools is provided in Chapter 3.

How to Use the In-Basket Exercises

Depending upon the purpose of the assignment, the instructor will determine if the assignment should be timed. Demonstrated below is an example of how each in-basket exercise in the recruitment category might be used (see chapter 4, category 1, p. 28).

1a. Special Education Teacher Recruitment
Individual Assessment:
Resources Needed: In-basket Exercise 1a

Instructor says: *"Staffing is a major component of any human resource management system. The system perishes, however, if you do not have a pool of applicants from which to choose. Identify the issue(s) and fully describe what action you will take."*

1b. Minority Teacher Recruitment
Group Task:
Resources Needed: In-basket Exercise 1b, flipcharts, markers, and chalkboard

Instructor says: *"The issue of equal opportunity, affirmative action and diversity is as hotly debated today as it has ever been. Any community-conscious progressive organization will mobilize its resources to secure a fair representation of the people it serves. The challenge presented in 1b is a common one and not unique to education. You have 45 minutes to discuss the issue and prepare a plan. Each group will then have 10 minutes to present its plan to the class."*

1c. Lack of Administrative Applicants
Individual Introspection/Whole Group:
Resources Needed: In-basket Exercise 1c

Instructor says: *"Read In-Basket Exercise 1c. Take 10 minutes to read and write your response. What environmental issues should be considered? Defend your answer."*

After 10 minutes, ask volunteers to respond and summarize on the board or flipchart the reasons given for and against readvertising.

1d. Statewide Search
Think—pair—share:
Resources Needed: In-basket Exercise 1d

Instructor says: *"In this exercise you will spend 5 minutes independently identifying the key issue in 1d and writing down steps you might take to solve the problem. Following the individual exercise, you will select and work with a partner to share your ideas and agree on a plan of action. I will let you know when the 5 minutes are up."*

1e. National Search
Take-Home Assignment:
Resources Needed: In-basket exercise 1e

Instructor says: *"In-basket exercise 1e is assigned for next class session. You may use any outside resource available to you to develop your* plan as requested by the superintendent. Your grade will be based on how thorough and complete your plan is and how realistic it is in terms of implementation."

1f. Offering Contracts to Recruits
Assessment:

Resources Needed: Copy of this publication for each student and notebook

Instructor says: *"For your exam this evening, you are to assume the role of CJ Castle. As you arrive at work, you find items "F" in Categories 1 through 7 and 9 through 11 in your in-basket. You will be given 2 hours to deal with as many as possible. You must first read all the items to determine their degree of importance as I am asking that you respond to the items in priority order. You should take whatever action is required to complete the exercise, e.g., if you are invited to give a speech, then draft it. You will be graded on 1) the order in which you handle the item (priority), 2) the identification of the issue, 3) the process you use to solve the problem, including the questions to be asked, 4) the thoroughness of your action plan, 5) the content of your response, and 6) the number of items completed. If information is incomplete, make realistic assumptions and let me know what those assumptions are. Are there any questions? You may begin."*

1g. Incentives for New Teachers
Group Project:

Resources: None

Instructor says: *"Choose one or two classmates to work cooperatively on a brochure to use for recruiting teachers to a district of your choice. The brochure should be a prototype displaying the type of information that would attract teachers to your school district, including, but not limited to, the information suggested in 1g. Be as creative as you wish. I will give you 45 minutes of class time to work on it tonight and the brochure will be due next week. Please bring copies for all students."*

As can be seen from the illustrations above, in-basket exercises can be used in a variety of ways.

Staff Development at the District Level

The authors believe that principals and assistant principals (as well as those planning to assume leadership roles in the future) will benefit by working through the in-basket exercises included in this publication. By doing so, participants will:

- Become more comfortable when dealing with HRM problems and issues
- Clarify building level and central office roles and responsibilities
- Achieve greater districtwide consistency in administrative response (as a result of reaching consensus on a course of action for the various in-basket exercises)
- Avoid pitfalls that could lead to costly litigation, bad publicity and/or labor tensions
- Update knowledge of state and federal laws
- Become more knowledgeable about the district's own collective bargaining agreement(s), board policies and unwritten expectations

In staff development efforts initiated at the district level, the authors recommend that an "insider" facilitate the sessions. The person should be knowledgeable about state and federal laws impacting HRM, as well as the collective bargaining agreement(s) of the district. In addition, knowledge of board policies, administrative regulations and current practice would be important. In most districts, this would be an administrator whose responsibilities include human resource management: e.g., Assistant Superintendent HR, Director of Human Resources. In small school districts, the superintendent may need to provide the leadership.

It is difficult to estimate the amount of time that should be allocated for those working through the in-basket exercises. However, based on the authors' experience while field-testing in graduate courses in HRM, it would be reasonable to allocate approximately 30 hours. This would allow 15 minutes (on the average) for each of the 120 in-basket exercises. It should be noted, however, that the amount of time required can be reduced significantly through "homework" and placing some time limits on discussion.

Evaluating (Scoring) Responses to the In-Basket Exercises

When the in-basket exercises are used for purposes of assessment, judgments as to quality of responses will need to be made. In this regard, the authors have not attempted to provide a listing of correct answers to the in-basket exercises. There is not a correct answer, per se, for the vast majority of in-basket exercises included in this publication. Determining what is a correct or appropriate response will be conditioned by several factors. Among them are:

- State laws vary and as a result will alter what constitutes an appropriate response in a given setting.

- The instructional emphasis, as determined by the instructor, will vary. For example, in preparing students for the in-basket exercises in Category 1, recruitment, the instructor may present what he/she deems to be very important information (literature) associated with this function. Similarly, the instructor may provide handouts or recommend selected reading in the area prior to asking students to respond to the seven recruitment in-basket exercises. In such instances, the instructor may be looking for predetermined knowledge of certain recruitment techniques and/or the ability to apply specific information to the exercises in question.

- In addition to the above, such factors as collective bargaining agreements, board policies, administrative regulations and the school district "culture" alter what is deemed an appropriate response when the exercises are used in a professional development program at the district level.

While the authors believe there is no universally "correct" answer for the vast majority of the in-basket exercises included in this publication, scoring within a particular context can be readily achieved. Evaluating (scoring) the responses of participants to the in-basket exercises during field-testing is described below.

First, it should be noted that field-testing occurred in multiple sections of a graduate level course in HRM offered by a selected university. Here the authors prepared a "model" or "ideal" answer for each of the in-basket exercises in advance. The model responses were appropriate for that particular setting. State and federal laws were cited as appropriate, as was the background information and contract language provided in this publication. In addition, information was utilized from course handouts (the authors had made plans to provide students with specific handouts associated with selected in-basket exercises in preparation for the course offering, e.g., what constitutes due process, sample reprimand, listing of state and federal laws, sample memo of understanding, etc.).

The model answers were subsequently used to score the answers provided by the students. In essence, the students' answers were compared with the model response. Depending upon the degree of precision desired, answers may be scored on a two–point "acceptable–unacceptable" basis or on a three– or five–point scale. For the most part, the authors utilized a five–point scale as illustrated below.

1. Superior quality
2. Above average quality
3. Average quality
4. Below average quality
5. Inferior quality

It is recommended that instructors score one exercise at a time (rather than one student's responses to several exercises). In this way, moving from one exercise to another does not distract the instructor. In addition, it is recommended that two readers be utilized whenever possible.

In scoring the responses, the authors read each of the responses and compared them to the model answer that had been prepared in advance. Responses were then placed in one of five groups, ranging from superior to inferior. Finally, all responses in each group were reread and adjustments were made, if necessary, to ensure consistency in scoring.

It should be noted that the "Suggested Questions" for each in-basket exercise helped facilitate scoring. The questions establish a framework to guide/aim the student toward the expected or desired response.

CHAPTER 3

The Setting

The exercises presented in this publication take place in the School District of the City of Melita. Melita is a middle-class city of approximately 75,000 residents. It is located in mid-America. The school district serves approximately 15,000 students.

Dr. Robert Eager is the superintendent of schools. He has held this position for the past 4 years. The school district is governed by a seven–member board, elected at large from the community. The district has 2 comprehensive high schools, a vocational-technical center, 5 middle schools, and 18 elementary schools.

Issues

The district has encountered some problems in recent years. It experienced some decline in student enrollment during the last decade. However, in recent years this trend has been reversed. Currently, the district is experiencing some growth. This is primarily a result of new housing developments in the northern region of the district. Melita is located 20 miles south of a major metropolitan area. A growing number of families have chosen to migrate to the northern part of Melita and commute to work in the larger city. This growth has been welcomed, even though it has resulted in some crowding of existing school facilities.

At the same time, the district is dealing with some old and deteriorating buildings. For example, Emerson Elementary, located in the southern region of the district, is nearly 70 years old and needs to be closed to students. It is the intent of the present administration to close the facility and absorb its students into the surrounding elementary schools.

Other problems encountered by the district include financial resources, student achievement levels and integration. The state legislature, 5 years ago, altered the way schools in the state are funded. The enacted legislation moved the primary source of revenue for school districts from property taxes to a statewide sales tax. This has resulted in a somewhat erratic level of funding for school districts. Student achievement and student/staff integration became very important issues in the district 4 years ago during the election campaign waged by candidates for vacant seats on the Board of Education. While the level of student achievement is at a respectable level in the district, the highest priority of the current school board is improved student performance. With respect to student/staff integration, the district has made considerable progress. Because of boundary changes, there are no racially identifiable schools. Similarly, progress has been made in recent years with respect to staff balance. Recruitment efforts have helped the school district assemble a teaching staff that is 20% minority.

Selected Demographics of Melita Public Schools

Students

As previously mentioned, the Melita Public Schools enroll 15,000 students. The racial composition of the enrolled students is as follows:

- 65% Caucasian
- 25% African-American
- 8% Hispanic
- 1% Asian/Pacific Islanders
- 1% Native American

Staff

The teaching staff of the school district is the largest single group of employees. The ethnic background of the teaching staff is as follows:

- 80% Caucasian
- 17% African-American
- 2% Hispanic
- 1% Asian/Pacific Islanders

The minority teaching staff is somewhat unevenly distributed throughout the district. Two elementary buildings are without minority representation in their professional ranks. However, 24 of the district's 26 schools have minority teachers on staff. The percent of minority teachers ranges from

8-30% in the 24 buildings with a minority staff presence. Overall, the district has 20% minority staff. This is up from 12% over the past 4 years. It should be noted that 70% of the teaching staff is female.

The support staff (custodians, bus drivers, secretaries, food services and maintenance workers, etc.) comprises the second largest employee group. This group is evenly divided male/female, and ethnically reflects the community at large, i.e., 32% minority.

Administration

There are 26 principals in the district. They, in turn, are supported by 20 central office positions. Secondary schools and two large elementary schools have the benefit of assistant principals. Secondary principals are mostly male, while the majority of elementary principals are female. Historically, the district has had a difficult time attracting female applicants to secondary principal and assistant principal vacancies. Overall, however, the administrative staff is evenly divided male/female. Twenty-four percent of administrators are minority.

Unions

A union represents teachers and almost all of the support staff. William Prime is the elected president of the teacher organization (Melita Education Association). He has served in this capacity for 7 years. The relationship between the MEA and the Superintendent/Board of Education has been somewhat combative of late, largely due to the lack of financial resources available to the school district.

Ronald Sullivan is president of the support (classified) staff union (Melita Support Staff Association). He has served in this capacity for 2 years.

Department of Human Resources

The Department of Human Resources is headed by Dr. CJ Castle, Director. The department also includes two supervisors, one who primarily works with the teaching staff and the second whose duties center around the support staff. The department also employs four secretaries, including Vivian Bergeron, the secretary to the Director.

Also available to Dr. Castle is Bruce Stoddard, a local attorney. Mr. Stoddard has been retained by the Board of Education to assist the district with legal matters, including those that confront the staff in the Human Resources Department.

It should be noted that, for the most part, the hiring practices of the district are decentralized. In the Melita Public Schools, principals and department heads hire their own staffs once applicants have been placed in a pool of eligible candidates by the Human Resources Department. For example, those seeking teaching positions with the district file applications with the Human Resources Department. The Human Resources staff assembles certification information, references, and background information. Once teacher applicants have been determined to be eligible for employment, they are placed in a pool. Principals are free to select their own teachers from the pool of qualified applicants. However, principals often must deal with district events such as enrollment fluctuations, attendance (boundary) changes and school closings that result in involuntary transfers of displaced staff. These resulting transfers, of course, restrict the principal's ability to hire his/her own staff.

The hiring of school administrators remains centralized.

Dr. CJ Castle

In the in-basket exercises presented in Chapter 4 of this publication, Dr. CJ Castle is the central figure. Those working through the exercises are asked to assume the role of the Director of Human Resources. Dr. Castle has been employed by the school district for 18 years: 8 years as a teacher, 4 years as an assistant principal, and 2 years as a Supervisor of Personnel Services before being promoted to Director 4 years ago.

A Central Office Organization chart for the school district is provided on the next page and is followed by directory information regarding the administrative staff as well as the school board.

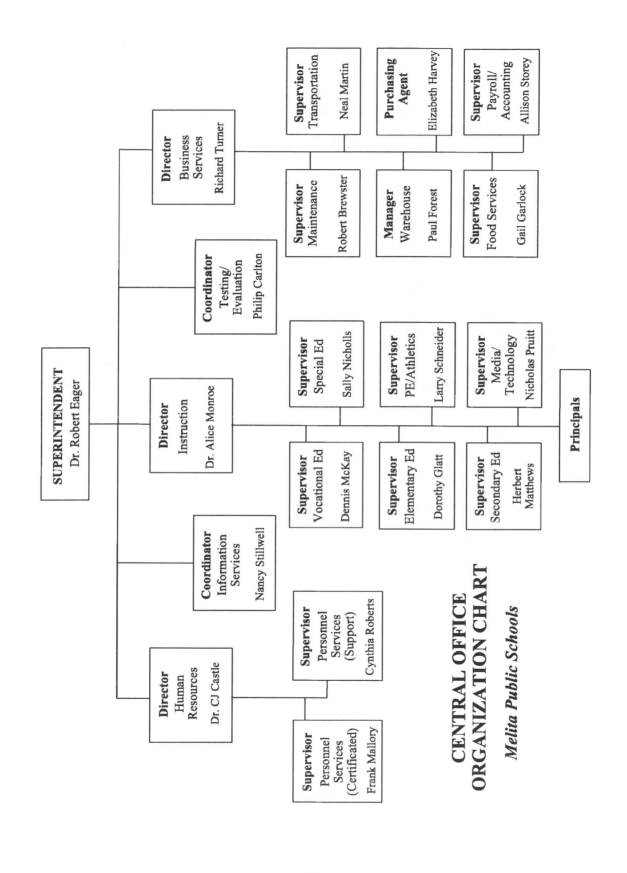

CENTRAL OFFICE ORGANIZATION CHART

Melita Public Schools

SUPERINTENDENT Dr. Robert Eager

Director Human Resources — Dr. CJ Castle

Supervisor Personnel Services (Support) — Cynthia Roberts

Supervisor Personnel Services (Certificated) — Frank Mallory

Coordinator Information Services — Nancy Stillwell

Director Instruction — Dr. Alice Monroe

Supervisor Special Ed — Sally Nicholls

Supervisor Vocational Ed — Dennis McKay

Supervisor PE/Athletics — Larry Schneider

Supervisor Elementary Ed — Dorothy Glatt

Supervisor Media/Technology — Nicholas Pruitt

Supervisor Secondary Ed — Herbert Matthews

Principals

Coordinator Testing/Evaluation — Philip Carlton

Director Business Services — Richard Turner

Supervisor Transportation — Neal Martin

Supervisor Maintenance — Robert Brewster

Purchasing Agent — Elizabeth Harvey

Manager Warehouse — Paul Forest

Supervisor Payroll/Accounting — Allison Storey

Supervisor Food Services — Gail Garlock

21

DIRECTORY

SCHOOL DISTRICT OF THE CITY OF MELITA

Board of Education

Allan Prescott, President

Michael Medler	Vice President	Joseph Baxter	Trustee
Arlene Dubay	Treasurer	Steven Boyd	Trustee
Linda Hutchins	Secretary	Barbara Turner	Trustee

Superintendent

Robert Eager, Ph.D.

Administrative Staff/Central Office

CJ Castle, Ph.D.	Director – Human Resources
Alice Monroe, Ed.D.	Director – Instruction
Richard Turner	Director – Business Services
Philip Carlton	Coordinator – Testing/Evaluation
Nancy Stillwell	Coordinator – Information Services
Robert Brewster	Supervisor – Maintenance
Gail Garlock	Supervisor – Food Services
Dorothy Glatt	Supervisor – Elementary Education
Frank Mallory	Supervisor – Personnel Services
Neal Martin	Supervisor – Transportation
Herbert Matthews	Supervisor – Secondary Education
Dennis McKay	Supervisor – Vocational Education
Sally Nicholls	Supervisor – Special Education
Nicholas Pruitt	Supervisor – Media/Technology
Cynthia Roberts	Supervisor – Personnel Services
Larry Schneider	Supervisor – Physical Education/Athletics
Allison Storey	Supervisor – Payroll/Accounting
Paul Forest	Manager – Warehouse
Elizabeth Harvey	Purchasing Agent

DIRECTORY
(Continued)

Administrative Staff (cont.)/Principals

High Schools

Michael McNair	Central
Raymond Tucker	McArthur
Julie MacDonald	Weaver Vocational/Technical

Middle Schools

Preston Roberts	Calumet
William Welters	Northern
Alex Bennett	Pioneer
Thomas Duncan	Rhodes
Jane Millard	Westerville

Elementary Schools

Rhonda O'Brien	Beech
Allen Truax	Eisenhower
Thomas Melvin	Emerson
Toni Seals, Ed.D.	Hillcrest
Kenneth Farr	Kennedy
John Ormon	Lakeview
Ronald Lentz	Lawndale
Ruth Osborne	Lockwood
Sandy van Horn	Logan
Roberta Egbert	Maple Ridge
Francis Cooper	Morrison
Evelyn Hughes	North Haven
Delores Wilson	Oak Ridge
Steven Michaels	Riverview
Terry Wagner	Sawden
Beverly Stewart	Trombley
Bert Williams	Willows
Sarah Smith	Woodlawn

CHAPTER 4

In-Basket Exercises

This chapter contains 120 in-basket exercises. The exercises have been grouped into 12 categories[1] as follows:

1. Recruitment
2. Legal/Policy
3. Selection/Credentials
4. Employee Relations/Public Relations/Counseling
5. Evaluation
6. Contract Administration
7. Collective Bargaining
8. Data Analysis/Budgeting
9. Investigations
10. Discipline
11. Planning (Staff)/Problem Solving
12. Grievance (Processing)/Arbitration

All related exercises have been grouped. Category 1, for example, contains seven exercises, all dealing with recruitment. This has been done to simplify the retrieval of desired exercises. Some exercises relate to more than one category. The user may choose to group the exercises in alternate ways to meet his/her unique objectives.

Participants are reminded that selected contract language from the collective bargaining agreements of the Melita Public Schools is provided in the appendices of this publication. Appendix A provides language governing the teaching staff, while Appendix B provides language associated with the support staff. The language is provided to assist those using this publication in a graduate course in HRM. In this setting, it is likely that participants will be coming together from numerous school districts and a common reference point should prove useful.

Those using this publication at the local district level as a professional development program may want to disregard the contract language

---

[1]Although staff development is not a major category, it should be noted that several in-basket exercises focus on staff development/training. Exercises 2b, 10j and 11i are obvious examples. In addition, exercises 3e, 3f, 4c, 5a, 5f and 10a have implications for staff development.

included in this publication. In professional development activities initiated at the district level, participants could be instructed to incorporate their own contract language and board policies when working through the in-basket exercises.

Suggestions to the Student

In working through the in-basket exercises, students are asked, "What action should be taken?" in response to each of the exercises. In responding to the in-basket exercises in an instructional setting, students should seek out relevant information when determining their course of action. Information sources include the following:

- The Internet
- The university library
- Handouts provided by the instructor
- Class notes (lecture and discussion)
- Contract language found in Appendix A and Appendix B
- Literature (suggested readings) associated with each category of in-basket exercises (e.g., recruitment)
- State and federal laws
- Description of the Melita Public Schools (Chapter 3)
- Practicing professionals in the field.

Students working through the exercises are encouraged to look beyond the symptoms and identify the real issue in each exercise. If information is incomplete, which it is likely to be, make realistic assumptions. If additional background information seems essential in order to determine "What action should be taken," students are asked to specify what steps they would take (what process they would go through) in determining a course of action. Many of the exercises offer opportunities to research current topics and practices in the field in order to prepare an acceptable response. Participants are encouraged to be exhaustive in their search for alternative solutions as both process and conclusion are important.

Particular attention should be given to the "Suggested Questions and Activities" which are provided for each of the in-basket exercises. They have been provided to guide those working through the exercises toward the expected or desired response, as well as stimulate discussion. The instructor may ask students to focus their attention on one or more of the suggested questions or pose additional questions. Some of the in-basket exercises include suggested activities. Again, the instructor may utilize the suggested activities or assign alternative activities.

Finally, the Web sites that follow are provided to assist students in their search for background information. During field-testing these Web sites were quite useful to students as they sought information to help them respond to the in-basket exercises.

www.mrsc.org/personnel/sexharr/sex/harr.htm

www.snc.edu/socsci/chair/336/home.htm

www.supremecourtus.gov

www.discriminationattorney.com

www.eeoc.gov

www.ahipubs.com

www.lawguru.com

Recruitment
1

1a. Special Education Teacher Recruitment

1b. Minority Teacher Recruitment

1c. Lack of Administrative Applicants

1d. Statewide Search

1e. National Search

1f. Offering Contracts to Recruits

1g. Incentives for New Teachers

(Also, see in-basket exercise 8c, p. 116)

MEMORANDUM

TO: CJ Castle, Director of Human Resources

FROM: Sally Nicholls, Supervisor of Special Education

DATE: December 15

SUBJECT: Upcoming Vacancies

I just wanted to let you know that I anticipate several vacancies in our department at the end of the school year. We are going to lose several people due to retirement and resignation. In addition, I anticipate some growth in the number of students we serve. We could have as many as 12 vacancies due to these factors. As you will recall we had some problems finding sufficient numbers of quality special education teacher applicants to fill our vacancies last year.

Do you think you could put together a plan whereby we could go out early and aggressively recruit qualified applicants? I would like to feel confident we would have ample certified candidates for these vacancies.

Please let me know what you think can be done. Thanks.

Suggested Questions/Activities:

1. How will you target special education teachers?
2. Develop an action plan to solve this problem, including any associated costs.

MEMORANDUM

TO: CJ Castle, Director of Human Resources

FROM: Robert Eager, Superintendent

DATE: December 16

SUBJECT: Minority Teachers

Last Friday when I addressed our teaching staff as part of our districtwide in-service day program, I could not help but notice how few minority teachers we have. With a student population that is approximately one–third minority, this simply is not acceptable. I know you and your staff have worked very hard on this. However, we simply must do more. The key here is recruitment. We have to get more minority teacher applicants. Would you put together a plan to address this problem?

Let's plan to meet next week to discuss. Please call my secretary and she will schedule a time. CJ, this is very important. I know if we work on this we can turn it around.

Suggested Questions/Activities:

1. Develop a plan to aggressively recruit minority teachers, including estimated costs.

IMPORTANT MESSAGE

FOR _____Dr. C_____

DATE _____April 11_____

M _____

OF _____

PHONE _____   _____   _____
           Area Code   Number   Extension

FAX _____   _____   _____
           Area Code   Number   Extension

CELL _____   _____   _____
           Area Code   Number   Extension

TELEPHONED	_____	**PLEASE CALL**	_____
CAME TO SEE YOU	_____	**WILL CALL AGAIN**	_____
WANTS TO SEE YOU	_____	**RUSH**	_____
RETURNED YOUR CALL	_____	**WILL FAX YOU**	_____

MESSAGE

Our deadline for applying for the assistant principal position at Westerville Middle School was yesterday. We have received only four applicants. Do you want to re-advertise or should I go ahead and schedule the interviews?

          Vivian

Suggested Questions/Activities:

1. What issues will impact your decision?
2. Respond to Vivian.

MEMORANDUM

TO: Dr. CJ Castle, Director of Human Resources

FROM: Dr. Robert Eager, Superintendent

DATE: April 16

SUBJECT: Middle School Assistant Principal Vacancy

I have thought about what you told me the other day regarding the lack of applicants for the assistant principal's position at Westerville. I don't think we have a choice. Would you go ahead and launch a statewide search? We simply have to have a large pool of qualified applicants from which to choose.

Please let me know your plans to attract candidates from outside the district.

Suggested Questions/Activities:

1. How will you increase the pool of applicants?
2. What steps will you take to initiate a statewide search?
3. Respond in writing to the superintendent.

MEMORANDUM

TO: CJ Castle, Director of Human Resources

FROM: Robert Eager, Superintendent

DATE: April 24

SUBJECT: Resignation of Director of Business Services

CJ, I wanted you to know right away that Richard Turner has decided to retire June 30. I knew he had been thinking about it, but I had hoped he would be with us for another year or two. This will leave a big hole in our operation.

I feel we must move quickly to find a replacement. Dick indicated to me that he did not feel anyone in his division was ready for this responsibility. In view of this, would you put together a plan for a national search? I feel we must go all out to find a top-notch person to head up our Business Division. I would like to have this person on board by July 1. Maybe we can talk next week regarding the specifics of your plan.

Suggested Questions/Activities:

1. What steps will you take to initiate a national search?

E-MAIL

FROM: SSmithprin@melita.K12.st.us
TO: CJCastlehr@melita.K12.st.us
DATE: May 3
SUBJECT: Offering Contracts to Recruits

Thank you for asking Toni Seals and me to cover the teacher recruitment fair at State University last Friday. It was great fun and we made contact with several candidates I would love to have in my building. Toni will be dropping off the resumes of those who we invited to the district for interviews. We told them your office would be calling them to schedule a date for their visitations.

Has the district ever considered offering contracts at recruitment events like the one at State University? There is a lot of competition (almost as many recruiters as recruits). This is particularly true with special education majors. Other districts hired many of them on the spot.

I feel we need to do something like this if we are going to be competitive. Let me know what you think.

Thanks again.

Suggested Questions/Activities:

1. What are the pros and cons of offering contracts on site?
2. How would you overcome any negative aspects of offering contracts on site?
3. Draft a contract that could be used for this purpose.

MEMORANDUM

TO: CJ Castle, Director of Human Resources

FROM: Alice Monroe, Director of Instruction

DATE: May 17

SUBJECT: Incentives for New Teachers

Last week at our principals' meeting, Preston Roberts mentioned that he was having problems landing the teachers he wanted for some of his vacancies. Apparently, he had offered positions to two individuals and had been turned down.

He said that one of our neighboring districts was helping new teachers with great deals on apartments. He did not know the details but believed the district had entered into some form of partnership with a couple of apartment complexes and as a result was able to offer their recruits a reduced rate. I am sure this would be attractive to new college graduates. In addition, he said he heard some districts in the southern part of the state were offering "signing bonuses" to new teachers in critical shortage areas.

Do you think we could do something like that? I told Preston I would relay this to you. You may want to give him a call.

Suggested Questions/Activities:

1. Brainstorm ideas that would entice new teachers to choose the Melita School District.
2. Prepare a flyer or brochure that can be used to recruit teachers, including a number of "perks." Be creative.

Suggested Readings

Recruitment

Barker, S. L. (1997, November). Is our successor in our schoolhouse? Finding principal candidates. *NASSP Bulletin*, 81(592), pp. 85–91.

Beebee, R. J. (1998). Recruiting and selecting new teachers: The recruitment budgeting cycle. *NASSP Bulletin*, 82(602), pp. 77–82.

Boody, R. & Montecinos, C. (1997). Hiring a new teacher? Ask for a portfolio. *Principal*, 77(1), pp. 34–35.

Darling-Hammond, L. (2001). The challenge of staffing our schools. *Educational Leadership*, 58(8), pp. 12–17.

Daugherty, M. K. (1998). A recruitment crisis: Strategies for affecting change. *The Technology Teacher*, 57(7), pp. 21–26.

Fielder, D. J. (1993, May). Wanted: Minority teachers. The *Executive Educator*, 15(5), pp. 33–34.

Futrell, M. H. (1999, May). Recruiting minority teachers. *Educational Leadership*, 56, pp. 30–33.

Gilman. D. A. & Lanman-Givens, B. (2001). Where have all the principals gone? *Educational Leadership*, 58(8), pp. 72–74.

Leonard, B. (2001). Recruiting from the competition. *HR Magazine*, 46(2), pp. 78–85.

Rodda. C. (2000, Jan./Feb.). Searching for success in teacher recruitment. *Thrust for Educational Leadership*, 29(3), pp. 8–11.

Starcke, A. M. (1996). Internet recruiting shows rapid growth. *HR Magazine*, 41(8), pp. 61–66.

Varma, G. (1997, Fall). Attracting the right talent: Prerecruiting ideas for new recruiters. *Journal of Career Planning and Employment*, 58(1), pp. 45–48.

Winston, M. (1998, May). The role of recruitment in achieving goals related to diversity. *College and Research Libraries*, 59(3), pp. 240–247.

Legal/Policy
2

LETTER

Dr. CJ Castle, Director
Human Resources
School District of the City of Melita

Dear Dr. Castle:

Enclosed you will find my resume and accompanying recent letters of recommendation. I was laid off in the recent downsizing of the staff at Melita General Hospital.

I believe that you will find my recommendations quite impressive. Apparently so did five of your principals as I have received a personal interview for every custodial position I have applied for. Unfortunately, I have not received an offer of employment—I attribute that solely to my age.

My employment history reflects exemplary attendance and quality of work; however, once the principal discovers that I am 71 years of age, he/she hurriedly provides a courtesy interview, and I am dismissed as quickly as possible. I am in excellent health and have no work restrictions.

I choose to bring this to your attention at this time, as it is not my desire to pursue an equal employment opportunity claim. I do feel, however, that such a claim would have merit.

I am looking forward to hearing from you.

Sincerely,

John Waverly

John Waverly
(555-1701)

Suggested Questions/Activities:

1. What potential liability exists for the Melita School District?
2. What secondary issues are there?
3. How will you handle this situation?

MEMORANDUM

TO: CJ Castle, Director of Human Resources

FROM: Robert Eager, Superintendent

DATE: August 14

SUBJECT: Sexual Harassment

As you are well aware, during this past school year, your department received 11 complaints of sexual harassment. As I recall your investigations concluded that two were unfounded while nine had merit. You and your staff are to be commended for helping us work through these difficult situations.

In my discussions with the board, they have indicated a zero tolerance for sexual harassment in the workplace. Would you work with your staff and develop a plan to inform (again) the entire staff of the law (and board policy) on this matter? It is obvious to me that significant numbers of our staff still don't get it.

Let's plan to meet next week to review your plan.

Suggested Questions/Activities:

1. How will you inform the staff of the policy? What plan do you have to provide annual notice of the policy's provisions?
2. What components should be included in an effective policy?
3. Should consideration be given to an anti-harassment policy that includes sexual harassment?
4. What consideration should be given to a clause prohibiting harassment against sexual orientation?
5. Secure and critique copies of sexual harassment or anti-harassment policies.

MEMORANDUM

TO: CJ Castle, Director of Human Resources

FROM: Dr. Robert Eager, Superintendent

DATE: August 15

SUBJECT: Teacher Resignations in August

Yesterday I met with the Principals' Advisory Council. We had a very productive meeting but toward the end of the meeting, Toni Seals expressed her concern about teachers resigning just before the start of the school year. She indicated that these late resignations (well into the summer) interrupt the instructional program and make it very difficult to find a satisfactory replacement on such short notice. Apparently, she had three teachers resign this past summer.

CJ, is there anything we can do about this? The principals feel we need a policy on this. Some even thought a penalty of some sort would be appropriate. What are your thoughts on this? I feel they have a legitimate concern.

Suggested Questions/Activities:
1.   What reasons do teachers have for delaying their notification of resignation?
2.   How might the district solve this ongoing problem?

E-MAIL

FROM: DWilsonprin@melita.K12.st.us
TO: CJCastlehr@melita.K12.st.us
DATE: August 16
SUBJECT: Results of Interviews

Yesterday we concluded our interviews for the vacant first grade position at Oak Ridge Elementary. Assistant Principal, Tom Murphy, and first grade teacher, Ann Thomas, and I interviewed six finalists for the position. The selection team discussed the results of the interviews this morning. We are recommending Alice Wilson for the vacant position. I am excited about this. I think it will be neat to have my daughter in this building.

Suggested Questions/Activities:

1. Identify the problem.
2. What are the potential problems if Ms. Wilson hires her daughter?
3. Is it significant that this was a team recommendation?
4. How would you handle this situation?

NOTE

September 1

Dr. C.

I have discovered that one of our teachers has been overpaid since she was hired 7 years ago. She was inadvertently given credit for 3 years of teaching experience from another state twice. This error amounts to an overpayment of $6,300.

Attached for your information is the State Board regulation that requires "errors in the distribution of funds must be reconciled upon discovery." I have highlighted it for you.

I knew you'd want to know about this immediately.

Vivian

Suggested Questions/Activities:

1. Describe the steps you will take to resolve the error.
2. Prepare any correspondence required.

MEMORANDUM

TO: Dr. CJ Castle, Director of Human Resources

FROM: Neal Martin, Supervisor of Transportation

DATE: October 17

SUBJECT: Sexual Harassment

At lunchtime today Connie Kirby came in to see me. She is one of our drivers in the West Region. She told me that Ralph Evans, also a driver for us, has been "hitting on her" and that she has asked him to stop. She said he is always coming around and trying to touch her. She said she doesn't want to get him in trouble. She just wants him to leave her alone.

Can you give me a hand on this? I told Connie I would look into it, but I'm not sure exactly what I should do. Call me right away. Thanks.

Suggested Questions/Activities:

1. Would you direct Neal to handle the situation?
2. Should Connie be interviewed at the central office? What questions should be asked?
3. What follow-up steps will you take?

E-MAIL

FROM: NMartintrans@melita.K12.st.us
TO: CJCastlehr@melita.K12.st.us
DATE: October 23
SUBJECT: ***URGENT***—Ralph Evans

CJ, I just got a call from Connie Kirby. She said Ralph Evans is stalking her. She told me that last evening while she was walking her dog (approximately 8:00 PM) she saw a man sitting in his car on the street where she lives. As she approached, she saw it was Ralph Evans. She said she was so surprised and startled to see him. She lives on a cul de sac and there is no way he just happened to be in the area. She wants us to "get him out of her life."

Would you call me right away? Connie is very upset.

Suggested Questions/Activities:

1. What action will you take?
2. Should law enforcement personnel be involved?

E-MAIL

FROM: ROsborneprin@melita.K12.st.us
TO: CJCastlehr@melita.K12.st.us
DATE: November 19
SUBJECT: Drug Testing

This morning one teacher and two students reported to me that Rod Markham, teacher, has a strong smell of alcohol about his person and is uncharacteristically gregarious. I sent my assistant principal down to talk to him and give me his perspective, but I need to know how to handle this.

By the way, he is Arlene Dubay's nephew!!

Help!!

Suggested Questions/Activities:

1. Does the district have written procedures regarding the use of alcohol at work? Are there provisions for testing?
2. What constitutes reasonable suspicion in order to justify testing?
3. How will you direct the principal to handle this situation?

E-MAIL

FROM: SSmithprin@melita.K12.st.us
TO: CJCastlehr@Melita.K12.st.us
DATE: Nov 21
SUBJECT: Possible Discrimination Claim

CJ, I am writing to alert you to a potential problem here at Woodlawn. As you know, we had the final interviews for our math position last week. We have offered the job to Paula Butler, who just graduated from State University. We interviewed four finalists for the position, including George Stern. When he called this morning inquiring about the status of his candidacy, I told him we had offered the job to Paula Butler. He was very upset. He said, "I know Paula Butler and this is blatant age discrimination. You will be hearing about this." Then he hung up.

CJ, I thought you should know about this. Is there anything we need to do? Help!

Suggested Questions/Activities:

1. What constitutes age discrimination?
2. Draft a list of questions that must be answered to determine whether the district is vulnerable to Stern's claim of age discrimination.
3. What records and/or documents will be needed to investigate any formal charges of age discrimination?

E-MAIL

FROM: RTuckerprin@melita.K12.st.us
TO: CJCastlehr@melita.K12.st.us
DATE: December 15
SUBJECT: Arrest Report

One of my teachers reported to me this morning that he was picked up last night for a DUI and spent the night in jail. He is a social studies teacher and the school's soccer coach. What is protocol in this case? He took a personal day today, but I told him I would get back to him ASAP.

Suggested Questions/Activities:

1. Is a DUI an offense that requires disciplinary action?
2. Are there any extenuating circumstances that determine whether a DUI requires disciplinary action?
3. Develop a protocol to be used when this incident occurs.
4. If this were a shoplifting incident, would the same protocol apply?

MEMORANDUM

TO: CJ Castle, Director of Human Resources

FROM: Robert Eager, Superintendent

DATE: January 29

SUBJECT: Arrest Report

I understand that new employees are placed on the job pending receipt of their national criminal background check, which takes 4–6 weeks to process. CJ, please establish criteria that determines whether an employee is permitted to remain employed should convictions be uncovered.

This could be a volatile issue.

Suggested Questions/Activities:

1. Establish the criteria you will use. Your criteria should be able to withstand public scrutiny.

E-MAIL

FROM: ABennettprin@melita.K12.st.us
TO: CJCastlehr@melita.K12.st.us
DATE: February 10
SUBJECT: EEOC Complaint

CJ, I thought I should contact you right away. This morning I received an EEOC complaint. James Moore filed the complaint. I don't know if you were aware of it or not but he applied for the position we filled last fall in seventh grade science. He is claiming that he has been discriminated against because he is handicapped. We did interview him, but we thought Pat MacIntosh was a better candidate.

I have never received an EEOC complaint before. Would you call me? I am not sure how this should be handled.

Suggested Questions/Activities:

1. What is the EEOC and what is its purpose?
2. What federal law(s) applies to this claim? Discuss.
3. What data will you need to respond to the complaint?
4. What procedures should be established in the district so that information may be retrieved when necessary?

E-MAIL

FROM:	FCooperprin@melita.K12.st.us
TO:	CJCastlehr@melita.K12.st.us
DATE:	March 1
SUBJECT:	Arrest Report

I hired a new cafeteria worker several weeks ago. I understand that her criminal background check just received reveals that she was found guilty of shoplifting last year.

Can she continue to work? She is very dependable and a good worker.

Suggested Questions/Activities:

1. What criteria will you use to make your decision?
2. What action will you take?
3. Write a letter to the employee justifying your decision.
4. Why is it important to have written documentation of your decision in the personnel file?

District Advisory Council
Melita Public Schools

March 15

Dr. CJ Castle, Director
Human Resources
School District of the City of Melita

Dear Dr. Castle:

Last evening the District Advisory Council held its monthly meeting. While discussing the district's new drug education program, the idea of drug testing employees was discussed. Several of our members thought this would be a good idea. Some of our group would like to see all employees tested while others thought we should start with those hired from this point forward.

I am writing this letter to invite you to our next meeting. We are anxious to hear your views on this. Our next meeting is scheduled for April 13, at 7:30.

Sincerely,

Dorothy Bock

Dorothy Bock
Chairperson

Suggested Questions/Activities:

1. What federal legislation covers drug testing of employees and who is affected?
2. Do the same standards apply for testing current employees as opposed to pre-employment testing?
3. Debate the issue of testing all employees as opposed to starting with new employees.
4. If you decide to test employees for drugs, what steps will you take?
5. Write a position paper clarifying your views. Assume you have the superintendent's support for your position.

E-MAIL

FROM:	LStantontchr@melita.K12.st.us
TO:	CJCastlehr@melita.K12.st.us
DATE:	May 14
SUBJECT:	Alleged Bias

I just received your letter notifying me that I did not meet the interview score criteria to be considered for the assistant principal vacancy at North Haven. I wish to meet with you immediately regarding this. I will tell you in advance that I believe the interview committee was biased because of my race and that I anticipated this would happen.

Please contact me as soon as possible.

Suggested Questions/Activities:

1. What is the potential liability to the district?
2. What steps will you take to deal with this?
3. How will you show that the "interview score criteria" is valid and that the committee was not biased?
4. Role-play the meeting.

Equal Employment Opportunity Commission

May 24

Dr. CJ Castle
Director of Human Resources
School District of the City of Melita

RE: Martha Severs

Dear Dr. Castle:

This is to advise you that we have received a claim of age discrimination from the above individual. A copy of the complaint is attached.

Please provide the following documentation within 30 days from the date of this letter.

- The complete personnel file of Martha Severs, including all documentation related to her performance as a teacher.

- A list of all applicants for each teaching vacancy at Eisenhower Elementary School for the previous 3 years, including ages of each and the name and age of each teacher hired for each vacancy.

- A list of all teachers not recommended for reappointment by Principal Allan Truax for the previous 3 years, including the age of each.

- A summary of action taken by the Human Resources Department to respond to Ms. Severs' complaint.

If you have any questions, please contact me.

Very truly yours,

Miguel Rodriguez
Regional Director

(See In-basket Exercise Ref. No. 5e, p. 84)

Attachment

April 10

<u>Statement of Complaint</u>

I was arbitrarily dismissed after one year by the principal who said in writing that I was too old. His words were that I "obtained my degree later in life." I planned with other teachers and delivered many of the same lesson plans, but they were not "written up," as I was.

I was at school Monday through Thursday until 6:00 PM or later preparing lessons and attempting to provide reports requested by the principal and department head that were not requested of other teachers.

Martha Severs

Martha Severs

Suggested Questions/Activities:

1. EEOC will be looking for what?

Suggested Readings

Legal/Policy

Blair, J. (2000). Districts accused of shortchanging workers in Mississippi. *Education Week*, 20(6), pp. 1, 18.

Cohan, A., Hergenrother M., Johnson Y. M., Mandel L. S. & Sawyer, J. (1996). *Sexual harassment and sexual abuse: A handbook for teachers and administrators*. Thousand Oaks, CA: Corwin Press.

Dowling-Sendor, B. (1997, July). Policing nepotism. *The American School Board Journal*, 184(7), pp. 14–15.

Dowling-Sendor, B. (2000, March). Zero tolerance versus privacy. *American School Board Journal*, pp. 1–6.

Gittins, N. E. & Walsh J. (1991). *Sexual harassment in the schools: Preventing and defending against claims*. Alexandria, VA: National School Boards Association.

Hartmeister, F. (1997). Handling requests for job references. *The School Administrator*, 344(3), pp. 5–6.

Ladestro, D. (1991). Over 40 need not apply. *Teacher Magazine*, 3(3), pp. 28–29.

Miron, L. F. (1996). *Resisting discrimination: Affirmative strategies for principals and teachers*. Thousand Oaks, CA: Corwin Press.

Petzko, V. (2001). Preventing legal headaches. *Principal Leadership*, 1(8), pp. 34–37.

Risser, R. (1993). *Stay out of court: The manager's guide to preventing lawsuits*. Upper Saddle River, NJ: Prentice Hall.

Wright, J. (1994, March). Ready to meet new drug requirements? *School and College*, pp. 13–19.

Young, P. (1999). Legal implications for teacher selection as defined by ADA and ADEA. *Journal of Law and Education*, 28(4), pp. 517–530.

Selection/Credentials
3

MEMORANDUM

TO: Dr. CJ Castle, Director of Human Resources

FROM: Dr. Alice Monroe, Director of Instruction

DATE: July 17

SUBJECT: Job Description

CJ, as you are aware, we have been working toward the establishment of a new administrative position in our division. We would like to take our recommendation to the Board in two weeks to create the position of preschool coordinator. This recommendation should, of course, include a well thought out job description. Would you help us on this? Please give me a call so that we might set aside some time for this important project.

Thanks.

Suggested Questions/Activities:

1. What are the components of a legally defensible job description?
2. Share a sample job description for a comparable administrative position from your school district. Critique it in terms of question one.
3. Write a job description for preschool coordinator that meets legal requirements.

IMPORTANT MESSAGE

FOR ___Dr. C_____

DATE ___August 10_____

M _____

OF _____

PHONE _____ _____ _____
Area Code   Number   Extension

FAX _____ _____ _____
Area Code   Number   Extension

CELL _____ _____ _____
Area Code   Number   Extension

TELEPHONED _____   **PLEASE CALL** _____
CAME TO SEE YOU _____   **WILL CALL AGAIN** _____
WANTS TO SEE YOU _____   **RUSH** _____
RETURNED YOUR CALL _____   **WILL FAX YOU** _____

MESSAGE

Just wanted to let you know I have scheduled the interviews for the coordinator of preschool for next Thursday. I assume you are preparing the interview questions. If you can give them to me, I will type them up for the rest of the interview team.

Thanks.

Vivian

Suggested Questions/Activities:

1. Using the job description prepared in 3a, develop a set of questions that will elicit information about each candidate's fitness for the position.

E-MAIL

FROM: SMichaelsprin@melita.K12.st.us
TO: CJCastlehr@melita.K12.st.us
DATE: Monday, September 22
SUBJECT: Alice Tensley

Something happened today that I thought you should know about. I was talking with Alice Tensley. You will recall we hired her last May from State University to take that fourth grade opening we had. Anyway, she indicated she was in a big disagreement with the university about meeting graduation requirements. As you will recall she was doing her student teaching last spring when we offered her the job and was scheduled to graduate at the end of summer school.

We thought she would be fine to start this fall. In any event, something must have gone wrong. She seems to be confident that things will be resolved to her satisfaction. However, at this point she apparently has not graduated.

I thought I should bring this to your attention right away.

Please advise.

P.S. I know there is some lag time, but has her official transcript arrived at your office yet?

Suggested Questions/Activities:

1. Several issues here are cause for concern. What are they?
2. What action will you take?
3. Assume you learn from the university that Alice Tensley has not completed graduation requirements. Write her a letter documenting the action you are taking.

MEMORANDUM

TO: CJ Castle, Director of Human Resources

FROM: Michael Medler, Vice President, Board of Education

DATE: November 5

SUBJECT: Allen Truax

I recently heard that Allen Truax, principal at Eisenhower Elementary, will be retiring at the end of the first semester. I know that Kim Edwards will apply for this position. As you are undoubtedly aware, Kim has been an outstanding teacher for more than 20 years at Eisenhower. I would certainly hope that she will get full consideration for this vacancy. I can't imagine a more qualified applicant.

Suggested Questions/Activities:

1. Will you respond to this letter? If so, indicate your response.

IMPORTANT MESSAGE

FOR _____ Dr. C _____

DATE _____ March 13 _____

M _____ Bert Williams _____

OF _____ Principal at Willows Elem. _____

PHONE _____ _____ 555-1217 _____ _____
          Area Code   Number   Extension

FAX _____ _____ _____
          Area Code   Number   Extension

CELL _____ _____ _____
          Area Code   Number   Extension

TELEPHONED	_XX_	PLEASE CALL	_XX_
CAME TO SEE YOU		WILL CALL AGAIN	
WANTS TO SEE YOU		RUSH	
RETURNED YOUR CALL		WILL FAX YOU	

MESSAGE

Bert Williams called this morning while you were in your grievance hearing. He wants your help. Apparently, one of his teachers (Mrs. Gonzales) has been unable to pass the State Teacher Competency test. She passed all sections except English. He does not want to lose her. He said she does a wonderful job at the school and the parents love her.

He said there must be something that can be done. She is too good of a teacher to lose.

Vivian

Suggested Activities/Questions:

1. How serious is this problem?
2. What factors must be considered?
3. What is your decision?

MEMORANDUM

TO: Dr. CJ Castle, Director of Human Resources

FROM: Dr. Robert Eager, Superintendent

DATE: June 3

SUBJECT: Board Interviews

As you know, I plan to involve two members of the board next week when we have the final interviews for the Director of Business Services position. The last time I involved the board in interviews, I felt they asked some questions that were inappropriate.

Would you plan to join me next Friday at 2:30 PM when I meet with board members Dubay and Medler? I think it would be wise for you to brief them on the interview process as well as the kinds of questions that they should not ask!

Thanks.

Suggested Questions/Activities:

1. Develop a list of legal and illegal questions.
2. Why is the integrity of the interview important?
3. Develop a legally defensible interview process.
4. Role-play the briefing session with the board members.

E-MAIL

FROM: ROsborneprin@melita.K12.st.us
TO: CJCastlehr@melita.K12.st.us
DATE: June 14
SUBJECT: Interview Questions

_____

At our recent principals' meeting, one of the topics was hiring new teachers and the interviewing process. We would like to formally request that a bank of interview questions that correspond to teacher competencies be developed. We would be happy to assist with this process.

Suggested Questions/Activities:

1. What are teacher competencies?
2. Develop a list of teacher competencies with accompanying definitions of each.
3. Develop three questions for each competency identified above.

MEMORANDUM

TO: CJ Castle, Director of Human Resources

FROM: Robert Eager, Superintendent

DATE: June 20

SUBJECT: Administrative Selection

CJ, as we prepare to replace administrators that retire, I want to be sure we are replacing them with the very best people available. Would you review your department's selection procedures? As we have discussed, I feel we must look inside and outside the district for replacements. However, when we get down to the three or four finalists we must do everything possible to ensure we are hiring the best candidates.

Let's plan to meet on this after July 4. I am anxious to hear your ideas on how we might strengthen our administrative selection procedures.

Suggested Questions/Activities:

1. What are the components of a legally defensible hiring system?
2. What steps would you put in place to refine your system? Be specific.
3. Prepare an Executive Summary for the meeting with Dr. Eager.

Suggested Readings

Selection

Al-Rubaiy, K. (1993, August). Five steps to better hiring. *The Executive Educator*, 15(8), pp. 21–23.

Boody, R. L. & Montecinos, C. (1997, September). Hiring a new teacher? Ask for a portfolio. *Principal*, 77(1), pp. 34–35.

Competency assessment and staffing. (1996). *HR Focus*, 73(3), p. 5.

Hartzell, G. (1999, November–December). Interviewing administrative candidates: What to ask? *Book Report*, 18(3), pp. 12–14.

Huling, L., Resta, V., Mandeville, T., & Miller, P. (1996). Factors in the selection of secondary school principals. *NASSP Bulletin*, 80, pp. 57–64.

Ingersoll, R. M. (1999). The problem of underqualified teachers in American secondary schools. *Educational Researcher*, 28(2), pp. 26–37.

Leonard, B. (1995). Reference checking laws: Now what? *HR Magazine*, 40(12), pp. 57–62.

Lynch, D. W. & Hill, M. S. (1994, November). Future principals: Selecting educators for leadership. *NASSP Bulletin*, 8(565), pp. 81–84.

Martin, C. (1993). Hiring the right person: Techniques for principals. *NASSP Bulletin*, pp. 79–83.

Norris, G. & Richburg, R. W. (1997, November). Hiring the best. *American School Board Journal*, 184(11) pp. 46, 48 & 55.

Scherer, M. (2001). Improving the quality of the teaching force. *Educational Leadership*, 58(8), pp. 1–6.

Steller, A. W. (1994, May). Chart a course for selecting new principals. *Updating School Board Policies*, 15(5), pp. 1–3.

Trimble, S. (2000). The teacher applicant pool: What top administrators seek. *Principal Leadership*, 1(7), pp. 45–48.

Employee Relations/Public Relations
Counseling
4

4a.   Wellness Program

4b.   Unsuccessful Teacher Applicant

4c.   Career Counseling

4d.   Memo of Understanding

4e.   Minority Representation

4f.   Speech

4g.   Women in Administrative Ranks

4h.   Teacher Absences

4i.   Keynote Speaker

4j.   Media Questions

4k.   Employee Recognition Program

MEMORANDUM

TO: Dr. CJ Castle, Director of Human Resources

FROM: Dr. Robert Eager, Superintendent

DATE: July 9

SUBJECT: Wellness Program

In my discussions with the board, they have expressed an interest in establishing a wellness program for our employees.

I feel that we need to do everything we can to maintain a healthy work force. However, we need to know what employees are interested in and how we might go about meeting their needs. I am interested in learning your thoughts on how this might work.

Let's plan to meet on the 17th to discuss this important matter. Will 10:45 AM work for you?

Suggested Questions/Activities:

1. Research organizational wellness programs that have proven to be effective. Cite your sources.
2. How might such a program be initiated?
3. What will you propose to the superintendent?

LETTER

Sept 15

Dr. CJ Castle, Director
Human Resources
School District of the City of Melita

Dear Dr. Castle:

I am writing this letter to you because I need your help. I recently moved here to be close to my mother who is retired and lives in the community. At this point in her life she is alone and frankly needs my help. Since my relocation, I have been trying to secure a teaching position in the district. I don't know what I am doing wrong, but I have not been successful in landing a position. In fact, I have only had one interview.

I would like to meet with you. It would be greatly appreciated if you would look at my resume and give me some suggestions. I can be reached at 555-0812.

Sincerely,

Helen Carr

Helen Carr

Suggested Questions/Activities:

1. What action will you take?

E-MAIL

FROM: MEverettaprin@melita.K12.st.us
TO: CJCastlehr@melita.K12.st.us
DATE: October 20
SUBJECT: Career Goals

I would like to schedule an appointment with you to discuss my career goals. As you know, I applied for the principal position at Lawndale Elementary. I was very disappointed when I did not get the position. I understand that Ron Lentz is doing a good job and I am happy for him.

I just want to discuss my career goals with you. Maybe you can tell me what I should be doing. I don't want to be an assistant principal forever.

Suggested Questions/Activities:

1. Career counseling is an important part of Personnel Administration. What information will you seek before meeting with M. Everett?
2. Role-play the following two scenarios:
   a. M. Everett has excellent references and her principal considers her his right hand.
   b. M. Everett has been an assistant principal for 8 years. Her current principal has said she is not perceived as a leader by the staff.

MEMORANDUM

TO: Dr. CJ Castle, Director of Human Resources

FROM: Bill Prime, President MEA

DATE: Nov 22

SUBJECT: Memo of Understanding

As a follow-up to our conversation last week, I would be interested in establishing a "Memo of Understanding" regarding job sharing. You indicated that two teachers had approached you with the idea and in talking with my executive committee, they seemed to be supportive of the idea. I have some ideas on how it might work. I am sure you do as well.

Please give me a call so that we might schedule a time to discuss in detail. It would be my desire to enter into the "Memo of Understanding" before the end of this semester.

Suggested Questions/Activities:

1. Is the concept of job sharing a viable one for the classroom?
2. What issues should be included in a "Memo of Understanding"?
3. Develop a "Memo of Understanding" for job sharing to propose to Bill Prime.

National Association of African-American People (NAAAP)

January 10

Dr. CJ Castle
Director of Human Resources
Melita School District

Dear Dr. Castle:

I am writing this letter to bring to your attention a very serious matter at Oak Ridge Elementary School. Recently I had an opportunity to visit the school. Ms. Wilson was very gracious. During my visit she not only took time to describe the instructional program to me (goals, priorities, etc.) she also gave me a tour of the building which included looking in on several classrooms. During my visit, I did not see a single Afro-American teacher. I found this appalling.

Approximately 20% of the student body at Oak Ridge is Afro-American, yet there are no Afro-American teachers. I feel it is important that this situation be addressed immediately.

I thought you and Dr. Eager had made considerable progress in this area. Apparently, I was wrong.

Sincerely,

Bill Underwood

Bill Underwood
Chapter President

Suggested Questions/Activities:

1. How will you respond to Mr. Underwood?
2. How will you address the lack of African-American teachers at Oak Ridge Elementary?

MEMORANDUM

TO: Dr. CJ Castle, Director of Human Resources

FROM: Dr. Robert Eager, Superintendent

DATE: January 19

SUBJECT: NAAAP Banquet

I have been invited to speak at the NAAAP Banquet scheduled for January 29. However, Board President Prescott and I will be attending the State School Boards Association meeting that evening.

Would you fill in for me on this? I planned to talk about our mutual goals and our district's progress toward meeting those goals. Please confirm you can do this on the 29th and I will let Bill Underwood know that you will be attending in my place.

Many thanks.

Suggested Questions/Activities:

1. Develop a list of "mutual goals."
2. Prepare a written speech to present on the 29th.

REGIONAL ORGANIZATION OF WOMEN

April 19

Dr. CJ Castle, Director
Human Resources
School District of the City of Melita

Dear Dr. Castle:

As you are probably aware, we have a wonderful program for students highlighting career opportunities for women in the 21st century. Last week I had the opportunity to make a presentation about our program to all the principals in the school district.

The presentation went well and I thought the principals were genuinely interested in its possibilities. However, I could not help but notice that approximately half of your administrators are men. I was very surprised at this. I know the majority of teachers are female and I thought your administrative staff was as well.

Would you share with me the complete demographics of the district's professional staff? In addition, I would be interested in knowing what the district is doing to address the apparent underrepresentation of women in the administrative ranks of the district.

Sincerely,

Jill Johnson

Jill Johnson
Coordinator

Suggested Questions/Activities:

1. Prepare a written response to Jill Johnson.

MEMORANDUM

TO: Dr. CJ Castle

FROM: Bert Williams, Principal

DATE: May 1

SUBJECT: Vonnie Dolan

I am very concerned about Vonnie's continued absence due to the illness of her mother. I have discussed this issue with her throughout the last school year and my concerns are documented in writing.

When she was unable to return at the beginning of this school year, I encouraged her to take a years' leave of absence so that the students would have continuity. She returned in October, worked for 3 weeks, and was out again for 2 weeks. Since that time she has had intermittent absences averaging 2–3 days each month.

I believe these absences are negatively affecting the students in her class and there are substantial parent complaints. I am requesting that you proceed with whatever action is appropriate so that I can provide a continuous quality-learning environment for the students.

Suggested Questions/Activities:

1. How does the Family Medical Leave Act relate to this situation?
2. How will you deal with this situation?

LETTER

May 3

Dr. CJ Castle
Human Resources
School District of the City of Melita

Dear Dr. Castle:

Graduation at Weaver Vocational-Technical School will be held at 6:30 PM on May 30 at the school. Our graduates would be honored if you would be the keynote speaker for our graduation. Your presentation should be approximately 15 minutes long.

I and several of my classmates have heard you speak in our classes and know that you would be entertaining and inspirational.

We look forward to a positive response.

Sincerely,

Mary Ann Erickson

Mary Ann Erickson, Class President
Weaver Vocational-Technical School

Suggested Questions/Activities:

1. Prepare a written speech to present to the graduates on a subject you feel will be interesting and inspirational for them. Your paper should include a title page, three or four pages in the body and a reference page. The paper should be in APA format.

MEMO

TO: CJ Castle, Director of Human Resources

FROM: Nancy Stillwell, Supervisor, Information Services

DATE: May 11

RE: Media Questions

CJ, I need your help! I don't know how they found out about it, but the media is all over that incident at Westerville where a teacher and a student got into it. What should I tell them? They want to know what is going to happen to Mr. Mendoza. In addition, they have made inquiries as to the student's status.

Give me a call right away!

(See In-basket Exercise Ref. No. 9k, p. 131)

Suggested Questions/Activities:

1. What is your response to Nancy Stillwell?
2. Establish a protocol to use in situations such as this one.

MEMORANDUM

TO: CJ Castle, Director of Human Resources

FROM: Robert Eager, Superintendent

DATE: June 14

RE: Employee Recognition Program

CJ, as we start planning for a new school year, would you give some thought to establishing a formal Employee Recognition Program? I don't think we do enough of this. I think we should recognize our employees throughout the year for their hard work and dedication to the school district. The program should include all of our employee groups: teachers, the various categories of our support staff and administrators. Let's plan to meet on this before the end of the month.

Suggested Questions/Activities:

1. Research an article on employee recognition/rewards and present a 5-minute summary to the class. Write a one- to two-page summary of the article citing complete bibliographic reference at the top of the page. Copy your summary for the class.
2. What is the value of an employee recognition program?
3. Brainstorm ideas for recognizing employees.

Suggested Readings

Employee Relations/Public Relations/Counseling

Arnold, J. B. (1993, October). Family leave: It's the law. *American School Board Journal*, 180(10), pp. 31–34.

Clark, R. T., Jr. (2001). Past and future trends affecting K–12 Employment relations: A management perspective. *Journal of Law & Education*, 30(2), pp. 227–245.

DeLapp, T. (1996, January). Twenty tips to level the playing field in an interview with a news reporter. *Thrust for Educational Leadership*, 25(1), p. 27.

Gupton, S. L. & Slick, G. A. (1996). Highly successful women administrators: The inside stories of how they got there. Thousand Oaks, CA: Corwin Press.

Horowitz, H. A. (1992). New guidelines for medical examinations. *HR Focus*, 69 (7), p. 7.

Martini, Jr., G. R. (1991, June). Wellness programs: Preventative medicine to reduce health care costs. *School Business Affairs*, 57(6), pp. 8–12.

Pitcock, A. R. (2000, October–November). Employee assistance programs: Promoting a healthy work environment. *AASPA Perspective*, p. 6.

Terry, P. (1999–2000). Empowering teachers as leaders. *National Forum of Educational Administration and Supervision Journal*, 10E(3), pp. 1–7.

Tucker, P. (2001). Helping struggling teachers. *Educational Leadership*, 58(5), pp. 52–55.

Starcke, A. M. (1996). Building a better orientation program. *HR Magazine*, 41(1), pp. 107–114.

Welch, F. C. & Daniel, C. (1997). Staff development for classified staff: One school district's approach. *Journal of Staff Development*, 18(1), pp. 12–15.

Evaluation
5

5a.   Plan of Assistance

5b.   Teacher Competence

5c.   Management-By-Objective (MBO) Evaluation System

5d.   Discriminatory Teacher Evaluation

5e.   Termination

5f.   Assistance Requested

5g.   Missed Timeline

5h.   Staff Evaluation Procedures Outdated

E-MAIL

FROM: TSealsprin@melita.K12.st.us
TO: CJCastlehr@melita.K12.st.us
DATE: October 4
SUBJECT: Plan of Assistance

CJ, as you know Sally Jeffers has been floundering this year. This is her second year, but she just can't seem to manage her classroom. I have received two or three parent complaints. I have spoken to her and made several suggestions on how she might improve.

Last Wednesday I observed her again for over an hour and it is obvious she needs improvement in several areas. I feel that if she doesn't make significant improvement, I can't, in good conscience, recommend her for continued employment next year. I would like to put her on a formal plan of assistance. I need your help on this.

Would you give me a call so we can discuss this?

Suggested Questions/Activities:

1. What is a "plan of assistance"?
2. What should be included in a "plan of assistance"?
3. Develop a formal district assistance plan to present to the superintendent for use when teachers are experiencing serious performance problems and are not responding to school-based intervention. Include all pertinent information.
4. How would you advise Toni Seals?

E-MAIL

FROM: FCooperprin@melita.K12.st.us
TO: CJCastlehr@melita.K12.st.us
DATE: Monday, November 15
SUBJECT: Third Grade Teacher

I hate to bother you, but I just don't know what to do. Mrs. Selby, our third grade teacher just lost it this morning. She was taking her students to the Media Center and apparently, she got to the center with only half her students. (The other 14 were scattered all over the building.) She didn't realize that she only had half of her students until she was asked why three of her boys were outside.

I am afraid for the children's safety. Mrs. Selby is such a nice lady and has been with us for a long time. However, I am afraid she has just "lost it." Something has to be done. Can you help me with this?

Suggested Questions/Activities:

1. What steps might be taken in view of the situation? What are the pros and cons of each?
2. How will you advise Francis Cooper?

MEMORANDUM

TO: CJ Castle, Director of Human Resources

FROM: Robert Eager, Superintendent

DATE: February 3

SUBJECT: Evaluation of Our Administrative Staff

As you know, I attended the AASA conference in New Orleans last week. It was wonderful. The sessions were the best ever. In addition, I came back with lots of ideas.

I would like to see us change the way we evaluate our administrators. I attended a session on Management-by-Objective (MBO) and it seems like it would be perfect for us in this district. I feel it would be much better than our present system and frankly, a much better fit for what we are trying to accomplish.

Would you plan to meet with me next Thursday at 11:00 so we can discuss? I know it would take some effort on our part, but I feel it would be a giant step forward. I'm anxious to hear your thoughts on MBO as an evaluation tool.

Suggested Questions/Activities:

1. Using at least two references, write an executive summary on MBO. Use APA style to cite your references.
2. How could MBO be utilized for evaluation of administrators?
3. What process would you use to explore the possibility of revising the administrator evaluation system?

MEMORANDUM

TO: CJ Castle, Director of Human Resources

FROM: Michael Medler, Vice President, Board of Education

DATE: April 7

SUBJECT: Teacher Evaluation

Yesterday I received a call from Rev. Ruben Williams. He called to express his concern about the treatment of one of our minority teachers. According to Rev. Williams, Melvin Daniels received a very negative evaluation from his principal (Francis Cooper).

Rev. Williams went into considerable detail about the evaluation. He indicated that he thought the principal was discriminating against Mr. Daniels and was trying to force him out of the school. He also said, "It was not surprising that we don't have an adequate number of minority teachers if this is the way they are treated."

CJ, would you look into this right away? I assured Rev. Williams that we would not tolerate discrimination in this school district.

Suggested Questions/Activities:

1.   What steps will you take to resolve this complaint?
2.   What involvement will Michael Medler have in the process?

MEMORANDUM

TO: Dr. CJ Castle

FROM: Allen Truax, Principal

DATE: April 8

SUBJECT: Martha Severs, Teacher

Attached is documentation to support my recommendation not to renew Mrs. Severs' teaching contract for next year. As you can see, this recommendation is made with the support of my assistant principal.

Although Mrs. Severs has worked very hard to be successful, she has difficulty in the areas of planning for instruction and presentation of subject matter. As you know, she worked in the school lunchroom for many years prior to obtaining her degree. She obtained her degree later in life and I do not believe she had sufficient internship experiences.

I would appreciate anything you can do to help her find a position somewhere so she can continue to accrue benefits in our state retirement system.

Please call me if you have any questions.

Suggested Questions/Activities:

1. What inferences can you make from this letter?
2. Describe the action you will take.

MEMORANDUM

TO: CJ Castle, Director of Human Resources

FROM: Jane Millard, Principal

DATE: April 20

SUBJECT: Curtis Stevens

I am requesting assistance from the district level to work with Mr. Stevens to improve his teaching performance. Mr. Stevens is a veteran teacher with 13 years' experience in the Melita Schools. He was transferred here from Rhodes Middle School 3 years ago because of a boundary change.

Enclosed are copies of his evaluation for the past 2 years. As you can see, Mr. Stevens has shown only slight improvement in one area and his performance is still not at an acceptable level. There continues to be an excessive number of parental complaints.

Mr. Stevens is aware of this request.

Suggested Questions/Activities:

1. Should school districts have a formalized program for assisting teachers who are experiencing serious performance problems?
2. If yes, what should it include?
3. Write a letter to Mr. Stevens informing him that he will receive district assistance and explain the process. Your style of writing and tone of the letter is critical to the success of the performance intervention.

E-MAIL

FROM:	TMelvinprin@melita.k12.st.us
TO:	CJCastlehr@melita.K12.st.us
DATE:	May 3
SUBJECT:	Missed Timeline

CJ, I did a stupid thing. You know that I was planning to dismiss Andy Westbrook at the end of the year. Well, I am afraid that I missed the timeline for notifying him. The contract states that probationary teachers will be notified 60 days before the end of the school year, if they are not going to be recommended for employment the following school year.

The letter was typed. I planned to give it to him Friday after school. Unfortunately, I was tied up with a parent and by the time she left, he had already gone for the day. Is there anything that can be done?

Please give me a call.

Suggested Questions/Activities:

1. What options, if any, do you have for dealing with the missed deadline?
2. Are union officials likely to "forgive and forget" the missed deadline?

MEMORANDUM

TO: CJ Castle, Director of Human Resources

FROM: Gail Garlock, Supervisor, Food Services

DATE: May 10

RE: Staff Evaluation Procedures

Last month I completed all of the evaluations for our 26 food service building managers. In addition, I helped some of them with the evaluations of their food service workers. CJ, I am not satisfied with our current system. As you know, the forms and procedures have been in place for a long time. It is time for them to be completely revised. I think the criteria are out of date and it doesn't seem that we are asking the right questions. I would like to throw out our current evaluation system and start over. I am willing to assist in any way I can, but I am not sure of how we should proceed.

We need your help. Would you give me a call?

Suggested Questions/Activities:

1. Should performance evaluations be job specific? Why or why not?
2. What process will you employ to review and update the evaluation system for food service managers and workers?

Suggested Readings

Evaluation

Danielson, C. (2001, February). New trends in teacher evaluation. *Educational Leadership*, 58(5), pp. 12–15.

Falcone, P. (2001, April). Give employees the (gentle) boot. *HR Magazine*, 46(4), pp. 121–128.

Howard, B. B. & McColsky, W. H. (2001, February). Evaluating experienced teachers. *Educational Leadership*, 58(5), pp. 48–51.

Jones, R. (1997). Showing bad teachers the door. *The American School Board Journal*, 184(11), pp. 21–24.

Mayo, R. W. (1997, May–June). Trends in teacher evaluation. *Clearing House*, 70(5), pp. 269–270.

O'Neil, I. R. & Adamson, D. R. (1993, February). When teachers falter. *The Executive Educator*, 15(1), pp. 25–32.

Pekoe Jr., L. C. (1991, October). Expert evaluation. *The Executive Educator*, 13(10), pp. 39–40.

Peterson, K. D., Wahlquist, C. & Bone, K. (2001, February). Using more data sources to evaluate teachers. *Educational Leadership*, 58(5), pp. 40–43.

Sandham, J. L. (1998). In Anchorage, district sets out to involve parents in evaluation. *Education Week*, 18(14), pp. 1–11.

Santeusanio, R. (1998, February). Improving performance with 360 degree feedback. *Educational Leadership*, 55(5), pp. 30–32.

Sawyer, L. (2001). Revamping a teacher evaluation system, *Educational Leadership*, 58(5). pp. 44–47.

Sullivan, K. & Zirkel, P. (1999). Documentation in teacher evaluation: What does the literature say? *NASSP Bulletin*, 604(83), pp. 48–54.

Timperley, H. S. (1998). Performance appraisal: Principal's perspectives and some implications. *Journal of Educational Administration*, 36(1), pp. 44–58.

Contract Administration
6

6a.   Language Interpretation

6b.   Break-time for Part-time Staff

6c.   Teachers Covering Absent Teachers

6d.   Hire from Within (?)

6e.   Fair Labor Standards Act

6f.   Involuntary Transfer Procedures

6g.   Voluntary Transfer

6h.   Grievance Threatened

6i.   Vacancy (?)

6j.   Formal Reprimand

E-MAIL

FROM: RTuckerprin@melita.K12.st.us
TO: CJCastlehr@melita.K12.st.us
DATE: August 1
SUBJECT: Pending Transfer Request

CJ, I need your help. As you know, we have a teaching vacancy in our Math Department at McArthur High School. This vacancy results from Mike Stewart's resignation after he accepted a position with another school district.

I have received several requests for transfer from my existing staff. (This is probably because the teaching assignment is all upper level courses.) Anyway, the problem is this. Chad Miller has applied. He would be wonderful. He is a math major and a wonderful teacher. However, Jason Horvath has also applied. He is certified, but only has a math minor. The teacher contract says that I must give preference to the teacher with the most seniority. Jason has more seniority than Chad Miller. What should I do? Jason does a good job in his current assignment that consists of lower level math classes, but I just can't see him in this position. Chad Miller would be perfect for the vacant position.

Please advise.

Suggested Questions/Activities:

1. Identify the issues related to this problem.
2. How will you advise R. Tucker?

E-MAIL

FROM:	TSealsprin@melita.K12.st.us
TO:	CJCastlehr@melita.K12.st.us
DATE:	October 1
SUBJECT:	Breaks for Hourly Employees

The contract provides two 15–minute breaks for full-time support employees. I have two people who work 3 hours each day. Do they get a 15–minute break?

Suggested Questions/Activities:

1. How does contract language address this issue?
2. If the contract is not clear on this issue, how will you advise Toni Seals and how will you defend your decision?

Melita Education Association

October 4

Dr. CJ Castle
Director of Human Resources
School District of the City of Melita

Dear Dr. Castle:

Please consider this a request to bargain the requirement by principals that teachers give up their planning periods to cover classes of teachers who are absent. The principals have stated to me that despite efforts to hire substitute teachers for all vacant classrooms, it is frequently not possible.

This places an undue burden on teachers who must relinquish their rights by contract to a planning period. Please call me to establish a mutually acceptable time to meet.

Sincerely,

Bill Prime

Bill Prime
President

Suggested Questions/Activities:

1. What preliminary steps, if any, will you take prior to the meeting with Bill Prime?
2. a. Brainstorm ways to solve the problem and
   b. Discuss and list the constraints of each.
3. Identify the top three solutions in priority order that are most beneficial to the district.

IMPORTANT MESSAGE

FOR ___Dr. C___

DATE ___October 27___

M ___Paul Forest___

OF ___Warehouse Operations___

PHONE _____ _____ ___0469___
Area Code   Number   Extension

FAX _____ _____ _____
Area Code   Number   Extension

CELL _____ _____ _____
Area Code   Number   Extension

TELEPHONED	_XX_	**PLEASE CALL**	_XX_
CAME TO SEE YOU		**WILL CALL AGAIN**	
WANTS TO SEE YOU		**RUSH**	
RETURNED YOUR CALL		**WILL FAX YOU**	

MESSAGE

Paul Forest called while you were with Mr. Turner. He said he hired a person as a delivery person who had excellent references; the person has already quit his other job and worked for us for 3 days. The union just called and told him he was obligated to hire from within based upon seniority. He wants you to call him ASAP!!!

      Vivian

Suggested Questions/Activities:

1. Review applicable contract language.
2. How will you advise Paul Forest?
3. What organizational factors will you investigate to determine how this problem occurred?
4. How might you prevent similar situations from occurring in the future?

E-MAIL

FROM:	ROsborneprin@melita.K12.st.us
TO:	CJCastlehr@melita.K12.st.us
DATE:	December 7
SUBJECT:	Request for Compensation

CJ, I need your help. Gloria Rey, our office clerk here at Lockwood Elementary, came to me this morning and said she would like to be paid for the extra time she has spent lining up substitute teachers. She said she has spent approximately 83 hours since school started on this. She claims she has taken calls at home in the evening and in the mornings before school from teachers calling in sick and in addition, she said she spends a lot of her own time lining up the subs and working on their payroll.

CJ, I don't know what to say. I asked her to help on this last fall. However, I had no idea she was spending this kind of time on it or working at home.

What do I do about this? Help!

Suggested Questions/Activities:

1. Research the Fair Labor Standards Act and be able to discuss the overtime provisions and exempt and nonexempt status.
2. Does Gloria have a legitimate request? Why or why not?
3. What action will you take?

MEMORANDUM

TO: Dr. CJ Castle, Director of Human Resources

FROM: Dr. Robert Eager, Superintendent

DATE: March 3

SUBJECT: Closing of Emerson Elementary

As you are aware, the board will vote next week on closing Emerson Elementary. After talking with Board President Allan Prescott, I am confident they will support my recommendation to close the school. However, I am sure they will have questions regarding what will happen to the staff. Would you be prepared to address this issue? They need to be assured that the staff will be reassigned in an orderly fashion.

Thanks for your help on this.

Suggested Questions/Activities:

1. Closing a school is a major event and can be very distressing for employees. What issues will you address?
2. Prepare a report for the board and present it to the class.

MEMORANDUM

TO: Dr. CJ Castle, Director of Human Resources

FROM: Larry Schneider, Supervisor – Physical Education/Athletics

DATE: April 10

SUBJECT: Vacancy at Central High School

CJ, we have a big problem at Central High School. They have a vacancy in their English Department due to a retirement. We desperately need to get Jerry Hendricks into that building. As you are probably aware, he has been selected to be the boys' varsity basketball coach at Central High School. He currently teaches at Rhodes Middle School. If his teaching assignment remains at Rhodes, it will cause numerous problems. It would be much better if he could be transferred to CHS. He is certified in English and Social Studies so he is certainly qualified.

Would you give me a call on this? It is very important that we do everything we can to shore up the basketball program at Central. We need to get back to our winning ways.

Suggested Questions/Activities:

1. What potential problems could this situation create?
2. What advice will you give Larry Schneider?

MEMORANDUM

TO: CJ Castle, Director of Human Resources

FROM: Bill Prime, President MEA

DATE: April 15

SUBJECT: Denial of Transfer Request

I would like to bring to your attention a situation at Central High School. Jennifer Coles, a 20-year teacher in the district, recently applied for a transfer to Central High School. She requested a transfer into the position that Paul Bliss held before his retirement. As you are probably aware Paul taught in the English Department: three sections of English IV and two classes of English Literature. Principal Mike McNair has denied Ms. Cole's request for a transfer, claiming that the assignment is now two sections of English IV, two classes in English Literature, and one section of American History. This is ridiculous. What Principal McNair has done is add a class in Social Studies that Ms. Coles is not certified in to make way for a coach he wants in the building. He has manipulated the schedule so that Jerry Hendricks can apply for this assignment and take over the head basketball job. This is a blatant disregard for a 20-year teacher's transfer rights.

If this is not resolved immediately, I plan to file a grievance and go to arbitration, if necessary. This kind of abuse won't be tolerated when it violates the rights of a veteran teacher in the district.

Suggested Questions/Activities:

1. Clarify the issue raised by Bill Prime.
2. What is the principal's right to change the master schedule?
3. What obligation does the district have to the 20-year veteran teacher?
4. Since Bill Prime has put you on notice that this issue will be grieved all the way to arbitration, develop your argument to defend your position if the issue is not resolved.

LETTER

May 1

Dr. CJ Castle, Director
Human Resources
Melita Public Schools

Dear Dr. Castle:

I am writing to you because I need your help. As you are undoubtedly aware, I am on involuntary transfer status because of the closing of our school. With 23 years of seniority, I know I will be placed in another position. The problem is that I want to transfer to the English Department at McArthur High School. In reviewing the list of available vacancies, I do not find any English vacancies at McArthur. This is what I don't understand. I know that two teachers in the English Department won't be back next year. One is retiring and I am quite certain another will be resigning because her husband took a job upstate. I believe the principal is concealing the fact that he has vacancies because he does not want to accept a transfer. He plans on waiting until all the teachers to be involuntarily transferred are placed and then he can hire whom he wants.

Would you help me on this? I desperately want to be transferred to McArthur.

Sincerely,

Connie Root

Connie Root

Suggested Questions/Activities:

1. Is it possible that Connie Root's claim has merit?
2. How will you resolve this issue?

E-MAIL

FROM:	RLentzprin@melita.K12.st.us
TO:	CJCastlehr@melita.K12.st.us
DATE:	May 22
SUBJECT:	Employee Discipline

CJ, I don't like doing this, but I feel it has to be done. I have been having a problem with Brian Wallace. He can't seem to get to work on time. He has been late several times during this school year (two or three times during the fall). I talked to him about this and I thought things would be fine. However, last week he was late twice (about 15 minutes) and this morning he came strolling in about 20 minutes late. This has to stop. It simply isn't fair to the other teachers. I want to give him a formal reprimand.

Would you help me with this? I want to make sure it is done correctly. I am sure we will hear from the union, but I don't care. I want this placed in his personnel file.

Suggested Questions/Activities:

1. Does Brian's conduct warrant a formal reprimand?
2. What are the elements of an effective letter of reprimand?
3. Prepare the letter of reprimand and send it to R. Lentz.

Suggested Readings

Contract Administration

Anton, T. A. (1996, February/March). Modifying teacher tenure to regain public confidence. *Educational Leadership*, pp. 34–37.

Archer, J. (2000). Districts targeting teacher seniority in union contracts. *Education Week*, 19(31), p. 5.

Barrett, R. S. (1998). *Challenging the myths of fair employment practices*. Westport, CT: Greenwood Press.

Barrett, R. S. (ed.). (1996). *Fair employment strategies in human resources management*. Westport, CT: Quorum Books.

Benefits and pension administration. (1996). *HR Focus*, 73(3), p. 5.

Blair, J. (2000). Districts accused of shortchanging workers in Mississippi. *Education Week*, 20(6), pp. 1,18.

Essex, N. (2000). Fair hiring and firing. *American School Board Journal*, 187(4), pp. 32–34.

Essex, N. (2001, April). The limits of zero tolerance. *Educational Leadership*, 1(8), pp. 5–7.

Flynn, G. (2000, September). Does a new right make a wrong? *Workforce*, 79, pp. 122–123.

Headcount reduction and employee choice. (1993). *HR Executive Review*: Downsizing, 1(1), pp. 5–8.

Merrow, J. (2000, January). Teacher seniority: Benefit or barrier? *Principal*, 79(3), pp. 49–50.

Petzko, V. N. (1998). Preventing legal headaches through staff development: Consideration and recommendations. *NASSP Bulletin*, 82, pp. 35–42.

Weller, D. (2001). Department heads: The most underutilized leadership position. *NASSP Bulletin*, 85(625), pp. 73–81.

Collective Bargaining
7

MEMORANDUM

TO: CJ Castle, Director of Human Resources

FROM: Robert Eager, Superintendent

DATE: November 10

SUBJECT: Formation of Bargaining Team

CJ, I would like you to serve as chair of our administrative team as we prepare to start bargaining with the teachers this year. Richard Turner will, of course, work with you and represent the Business Division. Would you pull together your recommendations regarding additional team members and get their names to me right away? I am planning to have the board officially appoint our team at our next board meeting.

Thanks.

Suggested Questions/Activities:

1.   What criteria should you use to select bargaining team members?
2.   Recommend a team as requested by the superintendent.

MEMORANDUM

TO: CJ Castle, Director of Human Resources

FROM: Robert Eager, Superintendent

DATE: November 15

SUBJECT: Negotiations/Incentives

In my discussions with the board, they would like to see us do something different this year when we address teacher salaries. They would like to see us build into the salary schedule some incentives. Simply put, they don't want to put 3–3½% on the salary schedule and get nothing in return. What they would like to see is some money set aside to reward those who do a good job (those who get results). They want to be able to reward our very best teachers.

Would you give this some thought? Please feel free to work with Dick Turner on this. I am writing to you at this time so that there is ample time to develop proposals that we might use in the upcoming negotiations. Keep me informed of your progress.

Suggested Questions/Activities:

1. Research and present a 5–10 minute summary of an article on incentive (merit) pay. Provide copies of your one to two–page summary to the class. Complete bibliographic references should be given in APA style at the top of your summary.
2. Develop a proposal for the superintendent and board's approval to present to the union.

MEMORANDUM

TO: Dr. CJ Castle, Director of Human Resources

FROM: Robert Eager, Superintendent

DATE: December 10

SUBJECT: Upcoming Collective Bargaining

It is time that we started discussing with the board our upcoming negotiations with the Teachers' Association. I plan to have an executive session with the full board to kick off the process and at least start to identify some of their priorities.

Would you plan to join us Friday at noon for this luncheon meeting? I would like you to outline for them some of the things you routinely do in preparation for the bargaining sessions. CJ, it does not have to be lengthy, but I thought you should brief them on how we prepare for negotiations.

Suggested Questions/Activities:

1. It is critical that board members be well versed on their role in collective bargaining. Prepare a list of items (activities) you wish to share in response to the superintendent's request.

MEMORANDUM

TO: Dr. CJ Castle, Director of Human Resources

FROM: Michael Medler, Vice President, Board of Education

DATE: April 9

SUBJECT: Salary Survey

At our last board meeting, Mr. Prime, president of the Melita Education Association, indicated that our teachers are not paid a competitive wage. He said our teachers are not paid as well as teachers in neighboring districts. Would you do a survey of the other districts in our area to see how we stack up? I really would like to know the facts. Thank you in advance for your assistance in this important matter.

Suggested Questions/Activities:

1. Prepare a form to be used to collect data so that the data are accurate.
2. How will you collect the information? What are the sources of information?
3. Is salary the only variable of interest? If not, what else should be considered?
4. How can these data be used during negotiations?

MEMORANDUM

TO: CJ Castle, Director of Human Resources

FROM: Robert Eager, Superintendent

DATE: April 10

SUBJECT: Sabbatical Leave

The board chairman has requested that we develop a proposal to provide sabbatical leave for our teachers. My feeling is that the district must clearly benefit from the process.

Please prepare a proposal to include selection criteria as well as safeguards for a return on our investment. The full board needs to discuss this before we move forward.

Suggested Questions/Activities:

1. Define "sabbatical leave."
2. What is the criterion for granting leave?
3. Prepare a list of questions that must be answered by the proposal.
4. Develop a written proposal for the superintendent.

LETTER

May 13

Dr. CJ Castle, Director
Human Resources
Melita Public Schools

Dear Dr. Castle:

Has any consideration been given to providing a salary supplement to sponsors of the Future Teachers organization? I would think that of all the extracurricular activities that teachers sponsor, this organization would be one given high priority by the school district. Some remuneration should be given to those of us who don't coach!!!

Sincerely,

Ann Rowan
Teacher, Northern Middle School

Suggested Questions/Activities:

1. Make a list of activities for which teachers typically receive a salary supplement.
2. What criteria should be used to determine how supplements are distributed?
3. On what basis would you determine the amount of each supplement?
4. Ann Rowan's letter may violate what collective bargaining rule?
5. Respond to Ann Rowan.

MEMORANDUM

TO: Dr. CJ Castle, Director of Human Resources

FROM: Dr. Robert Eager, Superintendent

DATE: July 27

SUBJECT: Establishment of a Sick Leave Bank

CJ, I agree the teachers' union seems dug in on the idea of establishing a sick leave bank for their members.

Would you go ahead and draft some language that we might propose at the table. Feel free to work with Dick Turner and his staff on this. I certainly want to know the cost implications on this before we get it out there. When you are ready, let me know so we can go over your proposal.

Suggested Questions/Activities:

1. What are the components of an "employee sick leave bank"?
2. What are the conditions for membership and use of days from the bank?
3. Who will manage the bank?
4. Draft a proposal for a teachers' sick leave bank, including estimated costs.

MEMORANDUM

TO: CJ Castle, Director of Human Resources

FROM: Robert Eager, Superintendent

DATE: July 29

SUBJECT: Past Practice

The board continues to see the union's argument of "past practice" played on the local news and has asked for clarification of the concept.

Please be prepared to address this and share examples at the meeting scheduled for the 7th.

If you have any questions, give me a call.

Suggested Questions/Activities:

1. What is the concept of "past practice"?
2. What is its significance to management/labor relations?
3. Cite examples of past practice so the board fully understands the concept.

MEMORANDUM

TO: CJ Castle, Director of Human Resources

FROM: Robert Eager, Superintendent

DATE: August 12

SUBJECT: Support Employees–Bumping

There has been considerable lobbying of board members by members of the support union requesting changes in our contract to permit bumping during periods of layoff. This is a major philosophical shift and will require considerable discussion.

Please be prepared to discuss the issue—pros and cons—with the board at our strategy session scheduled for the 19th.

Suggested Questions/Activities:

1. What is the concept of "bumping"?
2. List the pros and cons of bumping.
3. Make a recommendation and defend it.

MEMORANDUM

TO: CJ Castle, Director of Human Resources

FROM: Robert Eager, Superintendent

DATE: August 16

SUBJECT: Impasse

Since we have declared impasse with our teachers' union, it is critical that we prepare for the next step. It will be important to present relevant market data to support our position on the monetary issues.

Please pull together the criteria you used in selecting other school districts to show comparable data as well as any private sector companies.

Let me know when you are ready to review the criteria with me.

Suggested Questions/Activities:

1. What criteria would be appropriate to guide the collection of comparable data?

Suggested Readings

Collective Bargaining

Abel, G. P. (1991, May). Equity, accountability and teacher negotiations in the '90s. *School Business Affairs*, 57(5), pp. 30–31.

Bolton, D. G. (2001). Better bargaining. *American School Board Journal*, 188(3), pp. 16–20.

Christmann, R. W. (1997, August). Getting behind pay-for-performance. *School Business Affairs*, 63(8), pp. 7–11.

Decker, R. H. (1991, February). Helping the board of education and negotiating team understand their roles in collective bargaining. *School Business Affairs*, 57(2), pp. 6–10.

Doyle, R. (1998, July). A better way to bargain. *American School Board Journal*, 179, pp. 22–24.

Eiler, E. E. (1991, February). When collective bargaining isn't working. *School Business Affairs*, 57(2), pp. 18–21.

Frombach, J. W., (1991, February). Negotiations—are you prepared? *School Business Affairs*, 57(2), pp. 14–18.

Glaser, J. P. & Tamm, J. W. (1991, December). Better bargaining. *The Executive Educator*, 13(12), pp. 22–25.

Goodwin, L. K. (1993, Summer). Win-win negotiations: A model for cooperative labor relations. *Public Manager*, 22(2), pp. 18–21.

Herman, J. J. (1991, February). The two faces of collective bargaining. *School Business Affairs*, 57(2), pp. 10–14.

Odden, A. & Kelley, C. (1996). *Paying teachers for what they know and do: New and smarter compensation strategies to improve schools*. Thousand Oaks, CA: Corwin Press.

Ramming, T. M. (1997, August). Alternative approaches to negotiating. *School Business Affairs*, 63(8), pp. 3–6.

Data Analysis/Budgeting
8

8a.   Exit Interviews

8b.   Grievance Analysis

8c.   Budget Development for Recruitment

8d.   Staffing Needs/Involuntary Transfer Analysis

8e.   Workforce Analysis Preparation

MEMORANDUM

TO: Dr. CJ Castle, Director of Human Resources

FROM: Dr. Robert Eager, Superintendent

DATE: July 21

SUBJECT: Resignations

CJ, when I was reviewing your board report last month I noticed what seemed to be a large number of resignations. Do we know why employees are resigning? Maybe it's normal, but it seems like we have too many people leaving the district. I know you do some follow-up, but should we have a formal exit interview so we know exactly why they are leaving?

Let me know what you think.

Suggested Questions/Activities:

1. What is the purpose of an "exit interview"?
2. How might exit interviews be useful?
3. What process would you recommend for exit interviews? How would you use the data collected?
4. Are there limitations to exit interviews?

MEMORANDUM

TO: CJ Castle, Director of Human Resources

FROM: Robert Eager, Superintendent

DATE: January 29

SUBJECT: Analysis of Grievances Filed during the Past Year

Last evening I was talking with Bruce Stoddard about our upcoming negotiations with the teachers. He said his law firm would be ready to help in any way it could again this year. One thing he did say was we should do a thorough analysis of the grievances filed by the teachers' union during the last year or two. He suggested such an analysis could point the way toward troublesome language in the contract that should be revisited.

CJ, this sounds like a good idea. Would you move forward with this? Feel free to call Bruce if you need to. I'm anxious to see the results of your analysis.

Thanks for everything you do.

Suggested Questions/Activities:

1. Describe the process you would use to complete this analysis.
2. List examples of Melita's contract language that may be ambiguous.

MEMORANDUM

TO: CJ Castle, Director of Human Resources

FROM: Robert Eager, Superintendent

DATE: February 13

SUBJECT: Recruitment for Fall

As a follow-up to our conversation last week, I have asked the board to amend our current budget and establish a teacher recruitment account for $12,500.

Per our conversation, I have told the board that the teacher recruitment budget will target minority teachers as well as special education teachers.

Would you put together a plan for this recruitment effort? I will be asking you to present your plan at the next board briefing session that is scheduled for February 24.

Suggested Questions/Activities:

1. What process will you use to develop your recruitment effort?
2. How will you target minority and special education teachers in your recruitment efforts?
3. Who will you use as recruiters?
4. What ideas do you have to attract teachers to Melita over other school districts?
5. Prepare a recruitment plan for presentation to the board.

MEMORANDUM

TO: CJ Castle, Director of Human Resources

FROM: Robert Eager, Superintendent

DATE: March 21

SUBJECT: Involuntary Transfer of Teachers

At our board meeting next month, I would like to start briefing the board regarding the boundary change that is needed between Rhodes and Northern Middle Schools. As you are well aware, we need to reduce the number of students who attend Northern by approximately 150 by changing the attendance boundary between Rhodes and Northern. I would like you to be ready to present our plan for transferring teachers from Northern to Rhodes. How many will need to be transferred? How will it work, etc.?

If you can handle this part, Richard Turner can speak to student enrollment projections and Alice Monroe can address any concerns regarding the impact on the curriculum. Our presentation to the board needs to alleviate their fears.

Let's plan on discussing this at the cabinet meeting next week.

Suggested Questions/Activities:

1. What information will you need to determine how many teachers must be transferred?
2. Prepare a written report describing how the transfers will take place. Include a time line for the process.

MEMORANDUM

TO: CJ Castle, Director of Human Resources

FROM: Robert Eager, Superintendent

DATE: June 14

SUBJECT: Federal Compliance Audit

Recently we were informed that the district is scheduled for a Federal Compliance Audit. It is my understanding that the audit will be primarily concerned with our use of federal funds. Therefore, the Business Division will be handling most of the preparation for this visitation. However, one item does fall to your department.

Their letter indicates they would like to review the most recent workforce analysis for the professional staff and the support staff. I would like to place this on the agenda for our next cabinet meeting and give you an opportunity to share with the cabinet what this entails. In this way, the entire cabinet will be more familiar with what is involved. I realize you normally don't complete this until after June 30. For our upcoming meeting I would like you to present an overview of the process and how you will be going about pulling together the information needed for the workforce analysis.

Thanks.

Suggested Questions/Activities:

1. What is contained in a "workforce analysis"?
2. How will you collect the data?
3. How will you summarize and present the data?

Suggested Readings

Data Analysis/Budgeting

Burckel, D., Watts, J. & Watts, O. (1999–2000). The buck really does stop in the principal's office. *National Forum of Educational Administration and Supervision Journal*, 17E(4), pp. 20–21.

Bray, J. W., French, M. T., Bowland, B. J. & Dunlap, L. J. (1996). The cost of employee assistance programs (EAPs): Findings from seven case studies. *Employee Assistance Quarterly*, 11(4), pp. 1–19.

Class size must be negotiated with teachers, Oregon court rules. (1991, April 10). *Education Week*, p. 2.

Creighton, T. (2001). Data analysis and the principalship. *Principal Leadership*, 1(9), pp. 52–57.

Diegmueller, K. (1991, April 17), Tight budgets escalate school labor tensions. *Education Week*, p. 14.

Mackey, B. C. & Uhler, S. F. (1990). How to take an early out. *American School Board Journal*, 177(3), pp. 27, 42.

Murray, G. (2000, April). Class size: Major implications for school leaders. *NASSP Bulletin*, pp. 108–113.

Pereus, S. C. (2000, May). Cut cost without cutting quality. *American School Board Journal*, p. 7.

Peterson, D. (2000, October). School-based budgeting. *ERIC Digest*, 64, pp. 1–5.

Slosson, J. (2000). Taming the budget process. *Principal Leadership*, 1(3), pp. 54–57.

Streifer, P. A. (2001, April). The "drill down" process. *The School Administrator*, pp. 16–19.

Urbanski, A. (1997, January 15). Merit pay won't work in schools. *Education Week*, p. 48.

Investigations
9

IMPORTANT MESSAGE

FOR ___Dr. C_____

DATE ___August 15_____

M ___Anonymous_____

OF _____

PHONE _____ _____ _____
          Area Code   Number   Extension

FAX _____ _____ _____
          Area Code   Number   Extension

CELL _____ _____ _____
          Area Code   Number   Extension

TELEPHONED	_____	**PLEASE CALL**	_____
CAME TO SEE YOU	_____	**WILL CALL AGAIN**	_____
WANTS TO SEE YOU	_____	**RUSH**	_____
RETURNED YOUR CALL	_____	**WILL FAX YOU**	_____

MESSAGE

While you were interviewing this morning, I received a very interesting call. About 10:30, a woman called and would not give her name. She said you better keep an eye on John Ormon, principal at Lakeview. She went on to say that last night while her husband went into Get-N-Go she waited in the car. While sitting there, Mr. Ormon pulled up in his car across the street. He got out and approached two men who were standing next to an abandoned gas station. With the streetlights on, she could clearly see Mr. Ormon give one of the men something and in return, the man gave Mr. Ormon something. She went on to say that this corner (Fitzgerald and Henderson) is notorious for drug trafficking and she knows Mr. Ormon is an addict and should not be around children.

Vivian

Suggested Questions/Activities:

1. How does your office treat anonymous information?
2. Would this complaint be sufficient to constitute "reasonable suspicion" for drug testing?
3. What action will you take?

E-MAIL

FROM:	RTuckerprin@melita.K12.st.us
TO:	CJCastlehr@Melita.K12.st.us
DATE:	September 22
SUBJECT:	Complaint by Mrs. Fedig

Today I received a complaint about one of my teachers. This a.m. Mrs. Fedig came in with her daughter Jennifer, who is an eleventh grader here at McArthur. Mrs. Fedig told me that last evening Jennifer told her that Mr. Stevens had been touching her inappropriately and had invited her to his apartment. Mrs. Fedig was outraged and wants something done about this right now.

I asked Jennifer to tell me what happened. She indicated that she is a work-study student and has been assigned to correct papers and keyboard for Mr. Stevens during his prep hour. She said that he is always trying to get close to her and brush up against her. She said she hadn't said anything about it to him but the other day he had tried to kiss her and had wanted her to go out with him next Saturday. She said this made her very uncomfortable and she wanted it to stop.

I want your advice on how to handle this one. Would you call me right away?

Suggested Questions/Activities:

1. Should the principal handle this situation? Why or why not?
2. What immediate steps will you take?
3. Will you allow Mr. Stevens to remain at school until the investigation is concluded?
4. What factors are critical to insure a fair and unbiased investigation of allegations?
5. If the charges against Mr. Stevens are founded, what action will you recommend to the superintendent?

LETTER

October 4

CJ Castle, Director
Human Resources
School District of the City of Melita

Dear Dr. Castle:

I am writing this letter because I would like to lodge a complaint. As you are probably aware, North Haven Elementary operates an after-school program for its students and the children of the staff at the school. The program runs from 3:00–5:30 PM each afternoon. It is a great program. I appreciate it very much. With my work schedule (9–5 each day), it is just great for my daughter Anna. I don't know what I would do without it.

The problem is this. I have it on good authority that the principal, Mrs. Hughes, has her son in the program and does not pay. She may be the principal, but she should be paying just like everybody else. I don't want you to use my name in this complaint. I am afraid Mrs. Hughes and the school will take it out on my daughter. I just want the situation corrected.

I am writing you this letter in confidence in hopes that you can correct this unfair situation.

Sincerely,

Jane Merdock

Jane Merdock

Suggested Questions/Activities:

1. How will you handle Merdock's request for confidentiality?
2. What steps will you take?
3. Will you handle a complaint against an administrator differently from complaints against other employees? Why or why not?
4. Will you respond to Merdock after an investigation? If so, how?

IMPORTANT MESSAGE

FOR ___Dr. C_____

DATE ___October 4_____

M ___Tom Melvin_____

OF _____

PHONE _____ _____ ___1400___
          Area Code   Number   Extension

FAX _____ _____ _____
          Area Code   Number   Extension

CELL _____ _____ _____
          Area Code   Number   Extension

TELEPHONED	_XX_	**PLEASE CALL**	_____
CAME TO SEE YOU	_____	**WILL CALL AGAIN**	_____
WANTS TO SEE YOU	_____	**RUSH**	_____
RETURNED YOUR CALL	_____	**WILL FAX YOU**	_____

MESSAGE

While you were in the budget meeting, I got a call from Tom Melvin, principal at Emerson Elementary. Apparently, he got a call from a Mrs. Watkins who is irate. She said when her son came home from school he told her Mr. Bowen (custodian at Emerson) used a racial slur when referring to her son and his friends. She wants him fired. She said if something isn't done immediately she is going to the superintendent, the board, and the newspaper. Tom asked her to give him a little time to look into it. Tom wants to know what you think he should do. He said he told her he would get back with her right away.

        Vivian

Suggested Questions/Activities:

1. How will you handle this investigation? Be specific.
2. If the allegations are founded, what information will you consider when recommending disciplinary action?

NOTE

October 27

Dr. C:

When I was going through the reports we got back from the FBI on the fingerprints we submitted on our new hires, two came back with arrest records.

1. Tim Anthony–arrested last year for breaking and entering

2. Gail Whitlow–arrested 5 years ago for larceny.

I knew you would want to see these right away.

Vivian

Suggested Questions/Activities:

1. What additional information will you need?
2. If the information in the note from Vivian is accurate, what action will you take?

E-MAIL

FROM: MMcNairprin@melita.K12.st.us
TO: CJCastlehr@melita.K12.st.us
DATE: November 15
SUBJECT: Complaint Against a Teacher

This morning, Mr. and Mrs. McDonald and their daughter Grace, a senior here at Central, came in to see me. They indicated they wanted to file a complaint against Ms. Cockeral, one of our science teachers.

Mr. McDonald went on to say that, Ms. Cockeral, according to his daughter, was teaching the test and as a result, several students scored as high as Grace. He said the result of this was that his daughter's standing in the class had been diminished and this would have a negative impact on the likelihood of her being awarded a scholarship.

At this point, I quizzed Grace at length as to what Ms. Cockeral allegedly had done in class. I was certain that Ms. Cockeral had only reviewed for the Comprehensive Skills Tests. However, Grace insisted that Ms. Cockeral had taught the actual test items.

I am not sure what to do with this. Ms. Cockeral is an excellent teacher. I can't believe she would use the actual test items as review material.

CJ, you should know that Grace is a brilliant student. She scores at the 99th percentile on everything. As for this impacting who gets a scholarship and for how much, I can't say for sure. However, we do use the results of the Comprehensive Skills Test to determine the recipients of our local (district) scholarships.

Please call me on this.

Suggested Questions/Activities:

1. How would you proceed to investigate these allegations?
2. If the charges are founded, what action will you recommend be taken against the teacher?

E-MAIL

FROM: REgbertprin@melita.K12.st.us
TO: CJCastlehr@melita.K12.st.us
DATE: December 1
SUBJECT: Cash Receipts

CJ, something has happened today that you should know about. Kay Andrews, our Food Service cashier, asked to see me after lunch. She said she had an opportunity to see the deposit slips for the cash receipts from our lunch program last week. She said that there is no way that they are correct. She did not accuse anyone of stealing money, but she said there is no way that the deposit slips are correct. She said we take in a lot more money than that. After I pressed her for an explanation, she would only say that she did not want to get anyone in trouble, but she was sure that cash was missing. What should I do? I have never dealt with a situation like this before.

Suggested Questions/Activities:

1. Who would you contact to assist you with this problem?
2. What steps will you take to complete this investigation?

LETTER

February 7

Dr. CJ Castle
Director of Human Resources
Melita Public Schools

Dear Dr. Castle:

I have never written a letter like this before but something has come to my attention that simply isn't right. I have learned through a very reliable source that Mr. McKay, supervisor of Vocational Education, is ripping off the school district. He routinely has his car serviced at the vocational school by students and does not pay anything for the service. I understand that students are working on his car and gaining valuable experience. However, it seems to me that he should at least reimburse the school account for materials used (oil, filter, etc.). I know he pays nothing. This is stealing. He should be fired. I only bring this to your attention because it is wrong.

Sincerely,

A Concerned Citizen

Suggested Questions/Activities:

1. What information is relevant to this situation?
2. Does the anonymity of the complaint affect what you do?
3. If you proceed, how will you handle this investigation?

IMPORTANT MESSAGE

FOR   Dr. C

DATE   April 20

M   Sgt. Owens

OF   Melita Police Department

PHONE _____

| Area Code | Number | Extension |

FAX _____

| Area Code | Number | Extension |

CELL _____

| Area Code | Number | Extension |

TELEPHONED	_XX_	**PLEASE CALL**	_XX_
CAME TO SEE YOU		**WILL CALL AGAIN**	
WANTS TO SEE YOU		**RUSH**	
RETURNED YOUR CALL		**WILL FAX YOU**	

MESSAGE

Called this a.m. Said he wanted to let you know that they arrested Nicholas Gear last night for "attempted sale of a controlled substance." He said you should call him back at 555–1938. (I believe that Nicholas Gear is one of our bus drivers.)

      Vivian

Suggested Questions/Activities:

1. Describe the steps you will take.
2. Does this incident justify "reasonable suspicion" to test Nicholas Gear for drugs?

MEMORANDUM

TO: Dr. CJ Castle, Director of Human Resources

FROM: Neal Martin, Supervisor of Transportation

DATE: April 27

SUBJECT: Employees Fighting

This afternoon as we were preparing for the 2:30 run, two of our drivers got into a fight. Mark Cody and Jesse Mathews got into a fight about something that apparently happened last night. I am not sure of the details. When I got there, Mark was on the ground bleeding badly from the nose and mouth. Jesse Mathews was standing over him. I managed to get them apart and had Herbert Winslow take Mark for medical treatment. I sent Jesse home for the rest of the day.

I have never had anything like this happen before. Would you help me sort this out? I am not sure of the procedure on this one.

Suggested Questions/Activities:

1. How will you conduct this investigation?
2. What disciplinary action will you recommend?

E-MAIL

FROM: JMillardprin@melita.K12.st.us
TO: CJCastlehr@melita.K12.st.us
DATE: May 10
SUBJECT: Teacher/Student Confrontation

CJ, we had a terrible thing happen today here at Westerville when we were dismissing students at the end of 7th period. Mr. Mendoza, our music teacher and Eric Davidson (student) got into a scuffle. There was a lot of name-calling and some chairs were tipped over. I don't know for sure what started it. My assistant principal said it might have been over something that Eric said or did to Mr. Mendoza's daughter Amy who is also a student here. In any event, Mr. Mendoza grabbed Eric and shoved him around. Mr. Mendoza was very upset. Since it was at the end of the day I had to let Eric catch his bus. I told Mr. Mendoza to go home and I would speak to him tomorrow.

What should I do? About 30 or 40 students saw this incident. I just can't believe this happened. Call me.

Suggested Questions/Activities:

1. How will you conduct this investigation?

E-MAIL

FROM:	JMillardprin@melita.K12.st.us
TO:	CJCastlehr@melita.K12.st.us
DATE:	May 20
SUBJECT:	Investigation

CJ, here are notes from my individual conferences with the two custodians in question.

Custodian 1 states that Custodian 2 has made sexual comments to her including, "Why don't you dump that boyfriend of yours. Try me and you won't need him." She said he shows up in her assigned cleaning area even though he is scheduled to clean in another part of the building. He has remarked on two separate occasions: "You look hot tonight." This has occurred over the last two weeks. She said she did not come forward right away because she thought he would stop and because she is a probationary employee and he is a long time employee.

Custodian 2 denies he made the comments to her. He said he did go to her area twice—once to get some special cleaning equipment she had on her cart and a second time to obtain a mop. He has worked here for seven years, and we have never had a complaint before.

Please advise on this.

Suggested Questions/Activities:

1. How will you proceed?
2. How will you resolve this complaint if there are no witnesses?

Suggested Readings

Investigations

Barbee, A. L. (1996, January). My child was abused. *The Executive Educator*, 18(1), pp. 25–27.

Cohan, A., Hergenrother, A., Johnson, Y. M., Mandel, L. S. & Sawyer, J. (1996). *Sexual harassment and abuse: A handbook for teachers and administrators*. Thousand Oaks, CA: Corwin Press.

Dowling-Sendor, B. (2000, June). Employee against employee: What to do when workers accuse peers of harassment. *American School Board Journal*, 187(6), pp. 20–21, 55.

Harrington-Lueker, D. (2000). When teachers cheat. *The School Administrator*, 11(57), pp. 32–39.

Klaas, B. S. and Dell'omo, G. G. (1991). The Determinants of disciplinary decisions: The case of employee drug use. *Personnel Psychology*, 44, pp. 813–835.

Klaas, B. S. and Wheeler, H. N. (1990). Managerial decision making about employee discipline: A policy-capturing approach. *Personnel Psychology*, 43, pp. 117–134.

Sheppard, B. H., Lewinski, R. J., & Milton, J. W. (1992). *Organizational justice: The search for fairness in the workplace*. New York: Lexington.

Shopp, R. J. (1997, May). How to investigate a sexual harassment complaint. *School Business Affairs*, 63(5), pp. 16–20.

Shopp, R. J. (2000). The principal's dilemma. *Principal Leadership*, 1(1), pp. 23–27.

Wesman, E. C. & Eischen, D. E. (1990). Due process. *Employee and Labor Relations*, Washington, D.C., Bureau of National Affairs, pp. 4–82.

Zirkel, P. A. (1999, May). Showing R-rated videos in school. *NASSP Bulletin*, pp. 69–73.

Discipline
10

MEMORANDUM

TO: Dr. CJ Castle, Director of Human Resources

FROM: Dr. Robert Eager, Superintendent

DATE: October 17

SUBJECT: Due Process

Yesterday Board Vice President Medler asked me about "due process" in employee discipline cases. I guess I gave him a rather general answer because he did not seem to be comfortable.

Would you give him a call and outline for him the steps we take to ensure that an employee accused of wrongdoing does in fact get due process in this district?

Many thanks.

Suggested Questions/Activities:

1. Define "due process" and why it is important when handling employee allegations of misconduct.
2. Describe the process used to insure employees receive due process.

IMPORTANT MESSAGE

FOR _Dr. C_

DATE _Oct 29_

M _Bill Underwood_

OF _NAAAP_

PHONE			
	Area Code	Number	Extension
FAX			
	Area Code	Number	Extension
CELL			
	Area Code	Number	Extension

TELEPHONED	_XX_	**PLEASE CALL**	
CAME TO SEE YOU		**WILL CALL AGAIN**	
WANTS TO SEE YOU		**RUSH**	
RETURNED YOUR CALL		**WILL FAX YOU**	

MESSAGE

He is outraged. One of Central's teachers argued with another teacher at the school and addressed her with a racial slur in the presence of students. All McNair did was give her an oral warning. He is going to the press if further action isn't taken against the teacher.

Vivian

Suggested Questions/Activities:

1. What steps will you take?
2. Did McNair exercise good judgment by issuing an oral warning? What factors might he have considered?
3. Should the superintendent override the principal's decision and render a more serious disciplinary action?
4. What consequences will result from 1) allowing the oral warning to stand, 2) issuing a formal written reprimand or 3) suspending the teacher for three days?

E-MAIL

FROM: DWilsonprin@melita.K12.st.us
TO: CJCastlehr@melita.K12.st.us
DATE: November 7
SUBJECT: Discipline

My guidance counselor just reported this incident to me:

One of the students came to school this morning wearing a jacket with a strong odor of cat urine. Students teased him throughout the homeroom period. As the student entered his first period class, the teacher, standing at the entrance to the room, smiled as the student entered and said, "meow, meow, meow." The student burst into tears and went to the guidance office.

How far can I go with this? This is a probationary teacher.

Suggested Questions/Activities:

1. Is due process different for a probationary teacher?
2. What action will you take?
3. If the allegations are confirmed, what disciplinary action will you recommend?

E-MAIL

FROM: NMartintrans@melita.K12.st.us
TO: CJCastlehr@melita.K12.st.us
DATE: December 13
SUBJECT: Investigation

It seems that Paul Dimon, bus driver, is at it again. I had two parent complaints today that he has been using Bible scriptures in an attempt to change students' behaviors. This is not the first time there have been complaints about this particular driver. He has been previously warned to avoid any reference to religion.

Please advise.

Suggested Questions/Activities:

1. What actions will you take?
2. If the allegations are confirmed, what disciplinary action will you recommend?

MEMORANDUM

TO: Dr. CJ Castle, Director of Human Resources

FROM: Bill Welters, Principal

DATE: February 9

SUBJECT: Eileen Gibson, Teacher

As you are aware, the state is requiring that teachers document evidence of prior experience teaching students with English as a second language or take 30 hours of instruction within the next year.

Enclosed is the documentation provided to me by Ms. Gibson on school stationery from her previous position at an elementary school in another state and signed by the principal. I have subsequently verified with the principal that at no time did Ms. Gibson ask him to write a letter for her nor is this his signature.

I believe this constitutes gross misconduct on the part of the teacher and may affect her employment with the Melita School District as well as her state certification.

Please proceed with whatever action is required.

Suggested Questions/Activities:

1. Describe the steps you will take to resolve this problem.
2. What disciplinary action will you recommend?
3. Write Eileen Gibson a letter for the superintendent's signature that includes the disciplinary action for this misconduct.
4. What obligation is there for this incident to be reported to state certification officials?

LETTER

March 21

Dr. CJ Castle
Director of Human Resources
School District of the City of Melita

Dear Dr. Castle:

I am the parent of a 10-year-old student at Oak Ridge Elementary School. On Wednesday, my son came home with bruises on his arm (pictures attached). He said he was "fooling around" with another student during physical education class and the teacher grabbed him by the arm, pulled him some distance, then used force to make him sit down.

I immediately took him to our pediatrician who verified the bruises were the result of pressure applied to his arm. We called the principal who agreed to meet with us early the next morning. When we arrived, the teacher was present and the principal proceeded to sing this teacher's praises. Mrs. Wilson never once reprimanded him for the physical abuse of my son. She proceeded to discuss only that my son is a behavior problem.

My husband and I are not satisfied with the disposition by the principal and I would like to meet with you. I can be reached at 555–5466.

Sincerely,

Mrs. Patricia Sutton

Suggested Questions/Activities:

1. Is the principal likely to be cooperative if she feels you are questioning her judgment?
2. During the meeting, the parents produced pictures of bruises on their son's arm and a doctor's report. What will you do?

MELITA EDUCATION ASSOCIATION

April 10

Dr. CJ Castle, Director
Human Resources
School District of the City of Melita

Dear Dr. Castle:

I take great exception to the behavior exhibited by Mr. Tucker during the recent grievance hearing. Had you not restrained him, I suspect he would have initiated a physical altercation.

I expect swift and appropriate disciplinary action to be taken as it would be against any member of the bargaining unit.

Very truly yours,

Bill Prime

Bill Prime
President

Suggested Questions/Activities:

1. How will you respond to Bill Prime?
2. Should administrators be held to the same standards as others?

MEMORANDUM

TO: CJ Castle, Director of Human Resources

FROM: Robert Eager, Superintendent

DATE: April 11

SUBJECT: Discipline

CJ, Bill Prime has spoken with me about Raymond Tucker's behavior during the grievance hearing. I know that he wrote you regarding this. I have also spoken with Tucker and told him I planned to issue a letter of reprimand for his inappropriate behavior.

Since you were present, please draft the letter for my signature.

Suggested Questions/Activities:

1. Write a letter of reprimand to Mr. Tucker for the superintendent's signature.

E-MAIL

FROM: NMartintrans@melita.K12.st.us
TO: CJCastlehr@melita.K12.st.us
DATE: May 25
SUBJECT: Drug Testing

CJ, Vivian gave me your message regarding the bus driver's drug test. As I understand it, these are the facts. The bus driver tested positive for drugs, equivalent to the painkiller Darvon. She has a history of back trouble and holds a prescription for Percoset, which is comparable to Darvon. I understand she forgot her prescription and borrowed a pill from someone else to relieve the pain.

CJ, given our zero tolerance for drugs, what should we do about this one? I'll be in my office until 5:30—call me.

Suggested Questions/Activities:

1. Do you need additional information? If so, what?
2. Given the facts, what is your recommendation for disciplinary action?

MEMORANDUM

TO: CJ Castle, Director of Human Resources

FROM: Toni Seals, Principal, Hillcrest Elementary

DATE: May 29

SUBJECT: Progressive Discipline

At our recent principals' meeting, a number of issues came up relating to handling discipline with our staff. A few of us old-timers recall that you conducted a workshop three or four years ago on progressive discipline. It would be very helpful if you would provide an update. Our next meeting is scheduled for June 16 from 1–4 PM. We would be glad to devote as much time as you need for your workshop.

Please let me know if you will be able to do this for us and how much time you will need for the workshop.

By the way, if you could prepare sample letters for us to have on file as a guide, it would be most helpful.

Suggested Questions/Activities:

1. Name and define the steps in "progressive discipline."
2. Identify the components of each step.
3. Must the steps be followed in order?
4. How would you document a concern that does not rise to the level of a reprimand?

Suggested Readings

Discipline

Bahls, J. E. (1998, March). Dealing with drugs: Keep it legal. *HR Magazine*, pp. 104–116.

Bahls, J. E. (1999, March). Handle with care. *HR Magazine*, pp. 60–66.

Falcone, P. (1997, February). The fundamentals of progressive discipline. *HR Magazine*, pp. 90–94.

Falcone, P. (1998, February). Adopt a formal approach to progressive discipline. *HR Magazine*, pp. 55–59.

Frase, L. E. & Downey, C. (1990–91). Teacher dismissal: Crucial substantive due process-guidelines from court cases. *National Forum of Applied Educational Research Journal*, 4, pp. 13–21.

Grier, T. B. & Turner, M. J. (1990). Make your charges stick. *The Executive Educator*, 12 (2), pp. 20–21.

Hartwell, T., Steele, P. & Rodman, N. (1998, June). Workplace alcohol testing programs: Prevalence and trends. *Monthly Labor Review*, pp. 27–34.

Kiechel, W. (1990, May). How to discipline in the modern age. *Fortune*, pp. 179–180.

Leap, T. L. & Crino, M. D. (1998, May). How serious is serious? *HR Magazine*, pp. 43–48.

Lindle, J. C. & Shrock, J. (1993). School-based decision-making councils and the firing process. *NASSP Bulletin*, 77, pp. 71–76.

Ramsey, R. D. (1998, February). Guidelines for the progressive discipline of employees. *Supervision*, 59, pp. 10–12.

Rhodes, D. (1998, October). Drugs in the workplace. *Occupational Health and Safety*, pp. 136–138.

Yandrich, R. M. (1996, June). A strategy for managing behavioral problems at work. *HR Magazine*, pp. 151–160.

Planning (Staff)/Problem Solving
11

11a.   Overstaffed

11b.   Technology

11c.   Minority Representation

11d.   Disability

11e.   Substitutes Unavailable

11f.   Possible Lay-Off

11g.   Positions to be Retained

11h.   Early Retirement Bonus

11i.   Future Administrator Development

11j.   Substitute Teacher Shortage

11k.   Teacher Training in Jeopardy

11l.   Teacher Absenteeism

E-MAIL

FROM: RTurnerbus@melita.K12.st.us
TO: CJCastlehr@melita.K12.st.us
DATE: September 1
SUBJECT: Staffing

CJ, Lockwood Elementary is overstaffed 8 hours on its custodial allocation.

Please bring this into compliance immediately.

Suggested Questions/Activities:

1.   How will you deal with the excess custodial hours at Lockwood?
2.   What steps will you take to prevent this situation from happening again?

AUTOMATION, INC.

September 28

Dr. CJ Castle
Human Resources Director
School District of the City of Melita

Dear Dr. Castle:

I hope you will seriously consider the attached information, including testimonials from school administrators throughout the state. Our automated teacher attendance reporting and substitute teacher scheduler is the premier system in the country.

No longer, do . . .

- school administrators need to spend hours on the telephone attempting to secure substitutes for their absent teachers
- substitute teachers have to wait by the telephone for calls to work
- clerical employees complete lengthy absence reports for each teacher.

Won't you call me today for a free, no obligation demonstration for you and your colleagues. In addition, don't hesitate to call any one of the school districts listed in the brochure for an unbiased opinion of our system.

Very truly yours,

Arlene LaMott
Regional Representative

Suggested Questions/Activities:

1. You have recognized that the current system needs to be overhauled for some time. What steps will you take to explore using an automated system?
2. Who will you involve in this process?

National Association of African-American People (NAAAP)

October 13

Dr. CJ Castle
Director of Human Resources
School District of the City of Melita

Dear Dr. Castle:

I am deeply concerned about the minority hiring practices in the Maintenance Department. While a large number of workers are African-American, there is not one minority foreman, even though there have been two new foremen hired in the past 6 months.

I would like to meet with you as soon as possible.

Sincerely,

Bill Underwood
Chapter President

Suggested Questions/Activities:

1. Respond to Bill Underwood.
2. How will you prepare for this meeting?

LETTER

November 4

Dr. CJ Castle
Director of Human Resources
School District of the City of Melita

Dear Dr. Castle:

I have worked as a plumber in the Maintenance Department for the past 11 years and have enjoyed my tenure with the Melita School District. I was injured in an automobile accident 6 weeks ago and had to have back surgery. My doctors have told me that I can no longer do the irrigation portion of my work as a plumber as it requires considerable digging. The supervisor of Maintenance told me that I no longer have a job if I cannot perform the duties of my position.

Even though my back injury is not work related, Dr. Castle, I believe that the school district owes me a job and should do something to help me. Don't my 11 years mean anything? I have been authorized to return to work in 2 weeks, but Mr. Brewster says I don't have a job to return to.

Please let me hear from you as soon as possible.

Sincerely,

Harry Shafer

Harry Shafer

Suggested Questions/Activities:

1. What will you do to assist Harry Shafer?
2. Prepare a two- or three-page paper summarizing the major components of the ADA and an organization's responsibility to employees.
3. Respond to Harry Schafer in writing.

E-MAIL

FROM: BStewartprin@melita.K12.st.us
TO: CJCastlehr@melita.K12.st.us
DATE: December 15
SUBJECT: Staffing

We are having great difficulty obtaining substitutes for custodians and cafeteria workers when our regular employees are out sick. I'd like to take care of this situation before it develops into union problems.

Can you help us with this? I know we are not the only school with this problem.

Suggested Questions/Activities:

1. What will you do to resolve this dilemma?

MEMORANDUM

TO: Dr. CJ Castle, Director of Human Resources

FROM: Dr. Robert Eager, Superintendent

DATE: January 14

SUBJECT: Possible Lay-off

With the news that we received yesterday from the State Department of Education regarding our funding level for the next year, I feel it is imperative that we prepare now for the worst. If the state does in fact reduce our level of funding by approximately $2 million next year, we simply cannot absorb this reduction. In view of the cuts we made last year with the support staff, I feel this round of cuts will impact the teacher and administrative ranks. It could impact 40 or so positions.

At our next cabinet meeting, we need to address this possible shortfall in our level of funding. I think we should discuss the process we will go through in identifying possible areas of reduction, as well as our initial thinking on areas that might be cut without destroying the instructional program. I don't know how much attrition we can anticipate. You will need to address that.

Let's meet next week on this. I am anxious to get your thinking.

Suggested Questions/Activities:

1. What process will you recommend to determine which staff will be affected by the reduction?
2. How will you determine anticipated attrition in administrative and teaching personnel?
3. What are your initial thoughts on areas to be cut that would have the least impact on the instructional program?
4. If the instructional program must be cut, what will you recommend? What is the potential backlash for each recommendation?

E-MAIL

FROM:	RTuckerprin@melita.K12.st.us
TO:	CJCastlehr@melita.K12.st.us
DATE:	January 16
SUBJECT:	Possible Reduction-in-force

Mr. McNair and I have discussed on several occasions the "what if" issues should reductions in force become inevitable at the high school level—case in point: the closing of Emerson. Something needs to be worked out so that a high school does not lose coaches and other sponsors of extracurricular activities that are vital to a high school program. I realize this presents a union problem, but it is something that must be addressed and, I might add, critical that we keep those who need to run our programs.

Let's get together to discuss this.

Suggested Questions/Activities:

1. Draft a position paper on why it is important to retain certain teachers who coach or sponsor an activity that is considered vital to the school's culture and identity.
2. What criteria will be used to identify the personnel who should receive special consideration?
3. Anticipating the long-held tradition of seniority in unions, how do you plan to implement exceptions to the seniority role?
4. Draft contract language to present to the union that provides for waiving the seniority role in the event of reductions in staff or a layoff in order to retain key staff members.

MEMORANDUM

TO: Dr. CJ Castle, Director of Human Resources

FROM: Dr. Robert Eager, Superintendent

DATE: January 18

SUBJECT: Early Retirement Bonus for Teachers

I was talking with Board President Allan Prescott last evening. In view of our budget outlook for next year, he suggested we consider an early retirement bonus for teachers. He feels that we should seriously give some thought to this because it could diminish our need to lay off teachers and pay unemployment.

CJ, would you let me know what you think about this. How could we structure it, etc.? I told Allan we would give the idea serious consideration. Thanks.

Suggested Questions/Activities:

1. Brainstorm ideas for early retirement incentives to minimize layoffs.
2. Discuss pros and cons of each.
3. Recommend two or three options for consideration.
4. What is organizational memory?
5. Discuss how early retirement incentives can negatively impact the organization.

MEMORANDUM

TO: Dr. CJ Castle, Director of Human Resources

FROM: Dr. Robert Eager, Superintendent

DATE: April 4

SUBJECT: Developing Future Administrators

I have given considerable thought to our discussion last week regarding the meager number of applicants we are receiving for administrative vacancies. I have read about other districts experiencing some shortages, but did not realize our own situation was so troublesome.

I feel we must address this situation immediately. Would you put together a plan for attracting and developing prospective administrators from our own ranks? We simply must have a large pool of qualified candidates to select from in filling our upcoming vacancies. With the growth we are experiencing, coupled with the projected retirements, we need to act on this. I am anxious to hear your thoughts on how we can enlarge our administrative applicant pool. We may have to grow our own.

Suggested Questions/Activities:

1. Brainstorm ideas to attract candidates for administrative positions.
2. Do principals in the district develop and maximize opportunities for their assistants to assume the principalship?
3. What role can staff development play in this effort?
4. Draft a plan to submit to Dr. Eager.

E-MAIL

FROM: BStewartprin@melita.K12.st.us
TO: CJCastlehr@melita.K12.st.us
DATE: April 19
SUBJECT: *URGENT*–Substitute Teacher Shortage

_____

CJ, we need two more substitute teachers this morning. We have three teachers attending the district in-service session on technology and one on personal business leave. I have these covered.

The problem is that three teachers have called in sick this morning. I can take one of the classrooms, but I can't find anyone else available on this short notice for the other two rooms.

Can you help me on this? The children will be here at 8:30.

Suggested Questions/Activities:

1. How will you solve Beverly Stewart's dilemma?
2. What long-range plan can you propose to alleviate this problem?

E-MAIL

FROM: AMonroeinstruc@melita.K12.st.us
TO: CJCastlehr@melita.K12.st.us
DATE: May 2
SUBJECT: Montessori Preschool

As you know, teacher training for the new Montessori preschool will begin in 2 months on weekends and throughout the summer in order to be ready for implementation this fall. The union has told the principal that he cannot require the teachers to attend training. We really need to resolve this issue as our training is already scheduled, and it is imperative that we proceed.

Will you take care of this for me? Let me know if I can help.

Suggested Questions/Activities:

1. How will you initiate discussions with the union? Montessori education is very specialized and to deliver what is promised, teacher training is essential.
2. What solutions will you propose to the union that are not cost prohibitive to the district?
3. What organizational communications problem does this dilemma represent? What can be learned from this example?

MEMORANDUM

TO: Dr. CJ Castle, Director of Human Resources

FROM: Dr. Robert Eager, Superintendent

DATE: May 13

SUBJECT: Teacher Absenteeism

Yesterday I visited Northern Middle School and had lunch with the principal. During lunch, Bill Welters shared with me his concerns about teacher absenteeism. He indicated that practically every day they have teachers out and it was very difficult to find adequate subs. He said that he understood the importance of our staff development activities that took teachers out of the building and did not want us to retreat on that front. However, he feels very strongly that we need to offer some incentive (or reward) for teachers who do not use their sick days. He thought some form of incentive would reduce our absentee rate substantially.

CJ, I know you have worked very hard to increase our pool of available substitutes. Do you think some sort of incentive for teachers would work in reducing our absentee rates? Please share your thoughts with me.

Suggested Questions/Activities:

1. Discuss the concept of providing incentives to reduce teacher absenteeism.
2. Research what other districts in the United States have done and whether their plans have decreased absenteeism.
3. Generate a number of options for consideration, including an estimated cost of each.

Suggested Readings

Planning (Staff)/Problem Solving

Ax, M., Conderman, G. & Stephens, J. T. (2001, January). Principal support essential for retaining special educators. *NASSP Bulletin*, 188(3), pp. 66–71.

Darling-Hammond, L. (2001, May). The challenge facing our schools. *Educational Leadership*, 58(8), pp. 12–17.

Jones, M. (1996). Four trends to reckon with. *HR Focus*, 73(6), pp. 22–23.

Kirkpatrick, R. (2000). Recruiting and developing candidates for principal. *NASSP Bulletin*, 84(617), pp. 38–43.

Laabs, J. J. (1996). Eyeing future HR concerns. *Personnel Journal*, 75(1), pp. 28–37.

Mohr, N. (1998, April). Creating effective study groups for principals. *Educational Leadership*, pp. 41–44.

Pitkoff, E. (1993, March). Teacher absenteeism: What administrators can do. *NASSP Bulletin*, 77(551), pp. 39–45.

Playko, M. & Daresh, J. C. (1993, Summer). Mentoring programs for aspiring administrators: An analysis of benefits to mentors. *Spectrum: Journal of School Research and Information*, 11(3), pp. 12–17.

Potter, L. (2001, March). Solving the principal shortage. *Principal*, 80(4), pp. 34–37.

Russo, A. (2001, January). No substitute for quality. *School Administrator* (1), pp. 6–17.

Sparks, D. (1999, October). There's no underestimating high-quality training. *The School Administrator*, p. 42.

Sulla, N., Ed.D. (2001, October). Redesigning the revolving door: Retaining good educators. *Inside Education*, 1(4), pp. 6–11.

Grievance (Processing)/Arbitration
12

12a. Board Member Orientation

12b. Grievance from Melita Education Association

12c. Grievance from Melita Support Staff Association

12d. Grievance from Melita Education Association

12e. Grievance from Melita Education Association

12f. Grievance from Melita Support Staff Association

12g. Grievance from Melita Education Association

12h. Grievance from Melita Support Staff Association

12i. Grievance from Melita Education Association

12j. Proceeding to Arbitration

12k. Arbitration Award

NOTE:

Eleven exercises are included in this category of in-basket activities. Eight are Level Two grievances, i.e., exercises 12b–12i. Participants are asked to prepare their dispositions for each of the eight grievances. These grievances have been denied at Level One (or expedited to Level Two). You are asked to prepare your disposition for each at Level Two of the grievance procedure.

MEMORANDUM

TO: Dr. CJ Castle, Director of Human Resources

FROM: Dr. Robert Eager, Superintendent

DATE: November 13

SUBJECT: Board Member Orientation

As you are undoubtedly aware, I have been putting together an orientation program for Barbara Turner since her election to the Board of Education. In our discussion last week, she indicated she would like to meet with you to get an overview of your departmental operations and specifically gain more insight on how grievances are handled. I explained to her that you hear grievances at Level Two. She said she understood that and just wanted more information on the process.

Would you give my secretary a call so that we might schedule this for Mrs. Turner?

Thanks.

Suggested Questions/Activities:

1. How will you describe the grievance process to Barbara Turner?
2. Role-play the meeting between CJ Castle and Barbara Turner.

GRIEVANCE REPORT FORM

Grievance Filed Against: Michael McNair, Principal
Central High School

Filed By: David Ross, Teacher

Date Grievance Occurred: December 5

Statement of Grievance: Grievant is a physical education teacher at Emerson Elementary who is to be reassigned due to its closing. Grievant has seniority over other physical education teachers. A physical education position is available at Central High School, but the principal will not accept grievant in position stating he needs a female teacher.

Relief Sought: Assign grievant to vacant position immediately, in accordance with contract.

David Ross
_____
Grievant

Bill Prime
_____
President—M.E.A.

Disposition:

_____
Director—Human Resources

Suggested Questions/Activities:

1. Does this constitute sex discrimination under Title VII or does this meet the test of a bona fide occupational qualification (BFOQ)?
2. What will your disposition be?

GRIEVANCE REPORT FORM

Grievance Filed Against: Roberta Egbert, Principal
Maple Ridge Elementary School

Filed By: Angela Bing, Custodian

Date Grievance Occurred: January 21

Statement of Grievance: Principal allowed the head custodian to be present during grievant's annual evaluation. The head custodian is a member of the bargaining unit.

Relief Sought: Set aside comments of the head custodian; complete new evaluation and cease and desist the practice of allowing head custodian to have any role in evaluation.

angela Bing
       Grievant

Ronald Sullivan
       President–M.S.S.A.

Disposition:

             Director–Human Resources

Suggested Questions/Activities:

1. What does the contract say about performance evaluation?
2. How will you dispose of this grievance?

GRIEVANCE REPORT FORM

Grievance Filed Against: Dolores Wilson, Principal
Oak Ridge Elementary

Filed By: Cecilia Stewart, Teacher

Date Grievance Occurred: March 14

Statement of Grievance: The principal denied the grievant's request for a leave of absence (letter attached) when similar requests have been granted in the school district.

Relief Sought: Grant grievant's request for leave of absence.

Cecilia Stewart
_____
Grievant

Bill Prime
_____
President—M.E.A.

Disposition:

_____
Director—Human Resources

Suggested Questions/Activities:

1. What does contract language say in regard to leaves of absence?
2. What additional information will you need?
3. How will you rule on this grievance?

ATTACHMENT

March 1

Dolores Wilson, Principal
Oak Ridge Elementary

RE: Leave of Absence

Dear Ms. Wilson:

My husband has the opportunity to be on assignment in Paris next year to complete his novel for his publisher. This is an opportunity, not only for him, but for me as well.

While I am reluctant to leave my school family, I respectfully request a leave of absence for next school year so that I can retain my seniority. After 11 years, you can understand my reluctance to give that up. I am convinced that my experiences will enrich my teaching and bring a global perspective to my classroom.

I would appreciate your favorable consideration of this request.

Sincerely,

Cecilia Stewart

Cecilia Stewart

GRIEVANCE REPORT FORM

Grievance Filed Against: Thomas Duncan, Principal
Rhodes Middle School

Filed By: Anna Weiss, Teacher

Date Grievance Occurred: April 11

Statement of Grievance: Grievant is in her third year of teaching. She received a generally favorable evaluation; however, principal noted her attitude was unsatisfactory. Principal failed to provide an explanation for his negative comments and did not respond to grievant's request in writing that he clarify his negative comment.

Relief Sought: Eliminate negative reference to grievant's attitude without sufficient documentation to support same.

Anna Weiss
Grievant

Bill Brime
President—M.E.A.

Disposition:

_____
Director—Human Resources

Suggested Questions/Activities:

1.   What information will you seek?
2.   How important is specific documentation?
3.   How will you dispose of this grievance?

GRIEVANCE REPORT FORM

Grievance Filed Against: Mr. Robert Brewster,
Supervisor of Maintenance

Filed By: Edward Simmons, et al., Painters

Date Grievance Occurred: April 21

Statement of Grievance: Supervisor of Maintenance subcontracted the painting of Rhodes Middle School cafeteria in violation of the contract.

Relief Sought: Cease and desist subcontracting. Compensate painters for overtime lost.

Edward Simmons
_____
Grievant

Ronald Sullivan
_____
President—M.S.S.A.

Disposition:

_____
Director—Human Resources

Suggested Questions/Activities:

1.   What does contract language specify relative to subcontracting?
2.   Has the district violated the contract? How will you rule?

GRIEVANCE REPORT FORM

Grievance Filed Against: Jane Millard, Principal
Westerville Middle School

Filed By: Denise Ballentine, Teacher

Date Grievance Occurred: April 22

Statement of Grievance: Grievant holds tenure and was passed over for a summer school science teaching position while a second–year probationary teacher was hired.

Relief Sought: Cease and desist hiring probationary teachers when tenured teachers are qualified and apply for positions. Provide grievant a summer school science teaching position at Westerville Middle School.

Denise Ballentine
_____
Grievant

Bill Brime
_____
President–M.E.A.

Disposition:

_____
Director–Human Resources

Suggested Questions/Activities:

1. Has the district violated the contract?
2. How will you rule in this grievance?

GRIEVANCE REPORT FORM

Grievance Filed Against: Mr. John Ormon, Principal
Lakeview Elementary School

Filed By: Shirley Owens and Donna Clark,
Food Service Workers

Date Grievance Occurred: May 15

Statement of Grievance: Principal announced 3 weeks of summer work in the cafeteria during a teacher workshop when only half the cafeteria staff was present. Two volunteers with less seniority than the grievants were hired.

Relief Sought: Set aside the hiring of less senior cafeteria workers and hire the grievants who have seniority.

Shirley Owens Donna Clark   _Ronald Sullivan_
      Grievant   **President—M.S.S.A.**

Disposition:

                                  Director—Human Resources

Suggested Questions/Activities:

1. Does the contract speak to summer work for support staff?
2. How will you decide this grievance?
3. Role-play this grievance with both sides presenting their arguments.

GRIEVANCE REPORT FORM

Grievance Filed Against: Beverly Stewart, Principal
Trombley Elementary School

Filed By: Clayton Morris, et al., Teachers

Date Grievance Occurred: May 28

Statement of Grievance: Principal entered into bargaining outside the recognized bargaining agent by meeting with faculty and establishing a faculty dress code.

Relief Sought: Cease and desist bargaining outside the recognized bargaining agent. Set aside dress code established in violation of the contract.

Clayton Morris
Grievant

Bill Prime
President–M.E.A.

Disposition:

_____
Director–Human Resources

Suggested Questions/Activities:

1. Are schools allowed to make decisions such as the dress code issue involving only their staffs and administration?
2. How will you decide the grievance?

Melita Support Staff Association

June 1

Dr. CJ Castle
Human Resources Director
School District of the City of Melita

Re: Frank Zapata, Security Guard *vs.* Robert Brewster, Supervisor of Maintenance

Dear Dr. Castle:

Please consider this formal notification that the Melita Support Staff Association is proceeding to arbitration on the above referenced matter.

We believe the contract is clear on this matter and we are very disappointed in your disposition.

Very truly yours,

Ronald Sullivan

Ronald Sullivan
President

Attachment

Suggested Questions/Activities:

1. When proceeding to arbitration, you must prepare a case to justify your decision. Prepare your arguments, including witnesses you plan to call.

GRIEVANCE REPORT FORM

Grievance Filed Against: Mr. Robert Brewster
Supervisor of Maintenance

Filed By: Frank Zapata, Security Guard

Date Grievance Occurred: May 15

Statement of Grievance: Supervisor of Maintenance refused to pay grievant the difference between his regular pay and jury duty pay when he was required to report for jury duty between 9:00 AM and 5:00 PM for three days.

Relief Sought: Make grievant whole for three days lost wages when he was required to report for jury duty.

Frank Zapata
Grievant

Ronald Sullivan
President–M.S.S.A.

Disposition: The grievant is a third shift employee whose regular shift ends at 8:00 AM. His requirement for jury duty did not conflict with his regularly scheduled work hours; therefore, the grievance is denied.

CJ Castle
Director–Human Resources

ARBITRATOR'S AWARD

Melita Support Staff Association vs.
School District of the City of Melita
June 11

ISSUE

Are the outside applicant's "qualifications, experience, and interview responses" superior to those of the grievant for the position of senior accounting clerk?

SUMMARY OF AWARD

A position for senior accounting clerk was advertised for 10 days in the manner prescribed by contract. Grievant was one of five chosen from 17 applicants to be interviewed. An applicant from outside was hired and has been working in the position for 3 months.

The Agreement between the parties requires that "the applicant whose qualifications, work experience, and interview responses are superior shall be offered the position." Agreement further states, "If . . . two or more current employee applicants are equally qualified, the employee applicant with the most in-district experience will be offered the position."

The position was offered to an outside applicant whose qualifications exceeded those in the position description. Her interview responses were deemed superior because of the manner in which she responded to the question, "Give us an example of a time when you had to work under pressure and tell us how you handled it."

The arbitrator rules that the applicant's bachelor's degree may not be considered since only 2 years of college are listed as a requirement. Further, neither the position qualifications nor the duties reflect the requirement to work under pressure. Therefore, the arbitrator finds in favor of the grievant.

Suggested Questions/Activities:

1. In view of the arbitrator's ruling, what action will you take?

Suggested Reading

Grievance (Processing)/Arbitration

Block, J. N. (1993, April). The process of arbitration. *Appraisal Journal*, 61(2), pp. 234–238.

Cozzo, R. (1998, July). Peaceful grievance resolution. *American School Board Journal*, 179, pp. 20–22.

Dunlop, J. T. & Sack, A. M. (1997). *Mediation and arbitration of employment disputes*. San Francisco, CA: Jossey-Bass.

Egler, T. D. (1995, July). The benefits and burdens of arbitration. *HR Magazine*, pp. 127–30.

Gould, W. B. (1993). *A primer on American labor law* (3rd ed.). Cambridge, MA: MIT Press.

Jackson, G. (1993). *Labor and employment law desk book*. Englewood Cliffs, NJ: Prentice Hall.

Long, S. (1999, August). Unfair arbitration agreement not enforceable. *HR Focus*, p. 3.

Lurie, M. L. (1999, November). The 8 essential steps in grievance processing. *Dispute Resolution Journal*, 54(4), pp. 61–65.

Marczely, B. (1998). Defending effective supervision in a litigious climate. *NASSP Bulletin*, 82(602), pp. 89–94.

McShulskis, E. (1996, September). Managing employee conflicts. *HR Magazine*, 41, p.16.

Rueben, A. (2001). The top ten judicial decisions affecting labor relations in public education during the decade of the 1990s: The verdict of quiescent years. *Journal of Law and Education*, (30)2, pp. 247–274.

Spelfogel, E. J. (1999, May). Mandatory arbitration vs. employment litigation. *Dispute Resolution Journal*, pp. 78–81.

Zirkel, P. A. (1991, November). The price of due process. *Phi Delta Kappan*, 73(3), pp. 259–260.

BIBLIOGRAPHY

Barclay, L. & York, K. (1999). Electronic communication skills in the classroom: An E-mail in-basket exercise. *Journal of Education for Business*, 74(4), 249–253.

Bender, J. (1973). What is typical of assessment centers? *Personnel*, 50(4), 50–57.

Brannick, M. T., Michaels, C. E. & Baker, D. B. (1989). Construct validity of in-basket scores. *Journal of Applied Psychology*, 74(6), 957–963.

Collins, E. T. (1990). Finding the right person for the job. *The American School Board Journal*, 177(7), 35–36.

Cummings, T. G. & Worley, C. G. (1993). *Organization development and change*. Cincinnati, OH: West Publishing.

Dukerich, J., Milliken, F. & Cowan, D. (1990). In-basket exercises as a methodology for studying information processing. *Simulation and Gaming*, 21(4), 397–411.

Engelbrecht, A. & Fischer, H. (1995). The managerial performance implications of a developmental assessment center process. *Human Relations*, 48(4), 387–404.

Gill, R. (1979). The in-tray (in-basket) exercise as a measure of management potential. *Journal of Occupational Psychology*, 52, 185–197.

Gomez-Mejia, L. R., Balkin, D. B. & Cardy, R. L. (1995). *Managing Human Resources*. Upper Saddle River, NJ: Prentice Hall.

Griffiths, P. & Goodge, P. (1994). Development Centers: The third generation. *Personnel Management*, 26(6), 40–43.

Hakstian, R. & Scratchley, L. S. (1997). In-basket assessment by fully objective methods: Development and evaluation of a self-report system. *Educational and Psychological Measurement*, 57(4), 607–630.

Holton, E., Bates, R., Seyler, D. & Carvalho, M. (1997). Toward construct validation of a transfer climate instrument. 8. *Human Resource Quarterly*.

Ivancevich, J. M. (1998). *Human Resource Management* (7th ed.). Boston, MA: Irwin/McGraw-Hill.

Ivancevich, J. M. & Matteson, M. T. (1993). *Organizational Behavior and Management*. Boston, MA: Richard D. Irwin.

Jones, R. & Whitmore, M. (1995). Evaluating developmental assessment centers as interventions. *Personnel Psychology*, (48), 377–388.

Kesselman, G., Lopez, F. M., & Lopez, F. E. (1982). The development and validation of a self-reported scored in-basket test in an assessment center. *Public Personnel Management Journal*, 2, 228–238.

Knowles, M. S., Holton, E. F. & Swanson, R. A. (1998). *The Adult Learner* (5th ed.). Houston, TX: Gulf Publishing.

Kolb, D., Lublin, S., Spoth, J. & Baker, R. (1994). Strategic management development: Using experiential learning theory to assess and develop managerial competencies. In C. Mabey and P. Iles (eds.), *Managing Learning*. London: Routledge.

Livingston, J. S. (1983). New trends in applied management development. *Training and Development Journal*, 37(1), 14–24.

Lopez, F. M. (1966). *Evaluating executive decision making: The in-basket technique*. New York, NY: American Management Association.

Mailick, S. & Stumpf, S. A. (1998). *Conceptual learning theory in the practice of management development*. Westport, CT: Quorm Books.

Montuori, L. A. & Kimmel, E. B. (1994). *Teaching conceptual complexity using an in-basket instructional design.* (ERIC Document Reproduction Service No. ED 346 082).

Schippmann, J., Prien, P., & Katz, J. (1990). Reliability and validity of in-basket performance measures. *Personnel Psychology,* (43), 837–859.

Taylor, M. D. (1990). *Assessment centers for hiring and development (MIS Report)*, 22(4), Washington, D.C.: International City Management Association.

Wendel, F. C. & Joekel, R. G. (1991). *Restructuring personnel selection: The assessment center method*. Bloomington, IL: Phi Delta Kappa Foundation.

APPENDIX A

SELECTED[1] CONTRACT LANGUAGE
FROM THE AGREEMENT BETWEEN THE
BOARD OF EDUCATION OF THE MELITA PUBLIC SCHOOLS
AND THE
MELITA EDUCATION ASSOCIATION

ARTICLE 1
PARTIES TO AGREEMENT

1.02-CERTIFICATION: Pursuant to the provisions of State Statutes, the Board of Education of the School District of the City of Melita recognizes that the Melita Education Association has been certified by the Public Employees Relations Commission as the sole and exclusive collective bargaining agent for all employees in the union described herein with respect to wages, hours and terms, and conditions of employment.

ARTICLE 3
NEGOTIATION PROCEDURE

3.06-IMPASSE: Impasse may occur only as provided for in State Statutes.

ARTICLE 4
GRIEVANCE PROCEDURE

4.01-DEFINITION: A grievance is defined as a claim by a teacher, by name, or a group of teachers, by name, that there has been a violation, misinterpretation or misapplication of any provision of this Agreement. A grievance shall be processed as hereinafter provided.

4.08-FORMAL GRIEVANCE PROCEDURES:

STEP I: A copy of the grievance shall be forwarded by the grievant to the Superintendent and to the Association at the same time the grievance is filed with the immediate supervisor. The immediate supervisor shall meet with the grievant, and his/her legal counsel or Association representative

---

[1]This appendix includes only selected contract language. The language provided herein is that which is considered necessary background information for those working through the exercises included in chapter 4 of this publication.

if the grievant so chooses, and attempt to resolve the grievance. Such meeting will require at least two (2) working days' notice and shall be held within ten (10) working days of the date of filing of the formal grievance. The immediate supervisor shall indicate the disposition of the grievance in writing within seven (7) working days of such meeting and shall furnish a copy thereof to the grievant, the Superintendent, and to the Association. In the event the grievant is not satisfied with the disposition of the grievance, or if no disposition has been made within the time limits as provided in Step I, the grievant may submit his/her grievance, as filed in Step I, to the Superintendent within ten (10) working days of the date of disposition or the expiration of time limits for a disposition.

Step II: The Superintendent shall meet with the grievant, and his/her legal counsel or Association representative if the grievant so chooses, within ten (10) working days of the date of filing, and attempt to resolve the grievance. The Superintendent shall indicate his/her disposition of the grievance in writing within seven (7) working days of such meeting and shall furnish a copy thereof to the grievant, the immediate supervisor, and to the Association. If the grievant is not satisfied with the disposition of the grievance at Step II, or if no disposition has been made within the time limits as provided in Step II, the grievant, with the approval from and representation by the Association, may submit the grievance to arbitration in accordance with the rules of the American Arbitration Association.

Step III: Submission of a grievance to arbitration shall be initiated by the grievant, his/her legal counsel or by his/her designated Association representative, by filing a written request with the American Arbitration Association and with the Superintendent within ten (10) working days of the date of the Step II disposition of the grievance or the expiration of time limits for a disposition. The disposition of the grievance made by the arbitrator shall be binding on both parties; providing that the arbitrator shall have no power to add or subtract from, modify or otherwise alter the terms of the collective bargaining agreement. The Board and the Association will share any information relative to the disposition of the grievance prior to or during arbitration.

4.09-EXPENSES: Each party shall bear its own expenses in connection with arbitration; provided, however, the Association shall share equally with the Board only those fees and expenses of the arbitrator and witnesses called by the arbitrator.

ARTICLE 5
TEACHING CONDITIONS

5.01-WORKDAY: The basic workday for teachers shall be seven and one half (7½) hours on all days when students are in attendance. On all teacher duty days and in-service days, the basic workday for teachers shall be seven (7) hours. Teachers will report at 7:30 AM when students are in attendance. Teachers will report at 8:00 AM on duty and in-service days. The workday for teachers shall include:

(a) A lunchtime each day equivalent to the student lunchtime, but not less than twenty–five (25) minutes. The teacher's lunch period shall be without direct responsibility for students.

(b) Each middle and high school teacher shall be given one (1) continuous planning/conference time of not less than one (1) instructional period per day. The length of the instructional period each day will be determined by the individual school's master schedule. Elementary school teachers shall have planning/conference time totaling not less than fifty (50) minutes per day or the equivalent on a weekly basis to include a minimum of thirty (30) minutes per teacher per day except in those cases where this provision would create a disruption of the instructional program. Such time shall be used for lesson preparation and for meeting other job description responsibilities.

5.03-CHANGE OF SCHEDULE, EMERGENCIES: In the event of an emergency or other unusual circumstances as determined by the principal or other immediate supervisor, a teacher's daily work schedule may be temporarily changed. When such a schedule change necessitates the loss of a teacher's planning/conference period, and no volunteers are available, the loss of planning/conference period shall be on a rotating basis.

ARTICLE 7
TEACHER AUTHORITY AND PROTECTION

7.022: Should a complaint be made by a parent/guardian, student or other individual, which may result in disciplinary action against a teacher, the teacher shall be notified of the complaint in writing, and given an opportunity to be heard prior to the taking of such action. During this period, there shall be no record of said complaint placed in the teacher's personnel file. Prior notice is waived where evidence available to the Superintendent indicates that the presence of the teacher may be detrimental to the well-being of students or the learning process. Upon request to the principal or other immediate supervisor, a teacher shall have the right of representation during investigatory meetings, conferences, and/or interviews, which may lead to disciplinary action. Nothing herein is intended to preclude the administrator's right to conduct a thorough and impartial investigation.

7.024: Any discipline of a teacher including reprimand, disciplinary suspension, or demotion while under a teaching contract or supplemental contact shall be only for just cause. Discharges and suspension for the purpose of investigation of charges, which might lead to dismissal, shall be only for just cause and shall not be subject to the grievance procedure. The decision of the District not to renew a probationary contract teacher shall not be subject to this section.

ARTICLE 8
NONDISCRIMINATION

8.01-NONDISCRIMINATION: The Board and the Association agree that the provisions of this Agreement shall be applied to all teachers without discrimination on the basis of religion, age, sex, marital status, disability, race, color, creed, national origin or political affiliation.

ARTICLE 10
GENERAL EMPLOYMENT PRACTICES

10.01-VOLUNTARY TRANSFER TO ANOTHER SCHOOL:

(1) Teachers requesting transfers should do so no later than the last day of teacher attendance for the school year. Requests for transfers must be renewed annually by teacher if continued consideration is desired.

(2) A list of open positions within the bargaining unit will be made available to the Association by the fifteenth (15th) of each month.

(3) Whenever any permanent openings within the bargaining unit arise, the District shall publicize the same by giving written notice of such vacancies to the Association. The Board agrees that, if qualified and certified, and subject to instructional requirements and student needs, the priority in filling such vacancies shall be on a basis of districtwide seniority within the following categories and the following order:

First, teachers requesting voluntary transfer,

Second, teachers on the involuntary transfer list,

Third, teachers requesting a return from other leave,

Fourth, teachers recalled from layoff.

10.02-SPECIAL PROVISION: The provisions in Sections 10.03 and 10.05 shall be implemented as described herein unless an instructional requirement or student need is identified. The Superintendent shall determine if a decision contrary to these provisions is in the best interest of the District. A copy of the principal's or supervisor's recommendation to the Superintendent for exemptions from Sections 10.03 and 10.05 shall be provided to any affected teachers and the Association at the time the recommendation is submitted to the Superintendent. The Superintendent shall notify all teachers affected by the determination in writing in accordance with the Instructional Staffing Calendar and guideline.

10.03-INVOLUNTARY TRANSFER TO ANOTHER SCHOOL:

(1) A transfer is a change from one building or site to another. A reassignment at the same school site is not a transfer.

(2) Transfers shall be made on a voluntary basis, whenever possible; however, correct and proper operation of the School District will necessarily require that involuntary transfers be made.

(3) Prior to determining involuntary transfers, employees shall be given an opportunity to volunteer.

(4) Involuntary transfers may be made in the event of a school closing.

(5) Involuntary transfers may be made to achieve a reduction in the number of teachers assigned to a school or program. Teachers selected for involuntary transfer shall be those with the least District seniority who hold certification and are assigned to teach at least 50% of the workday in the program being reduced.

(6) A list of teachers to be involuntarily transferred will be compiled by the Human Resources Department. Vacancy information shall be provided to these employees. Thereafter, employees shall indicate the positions, in order of preference, which they desire. Teachers who have the highest seniority and appropriate certification shall be placed first.

(7) If there are no vacancies in the teacher's area of certification, the teacher shall be placed in the position of the least senior teacher with the appropriate area of certification and teaching assignment. In no event

shall an involuntary transfer teacher replace a teacher who has greater seniority. The teacher of second highest seniority ranking in a certification area shall be placed next, and so on until all teachers are placed.

(8) New teachers in a specific subject area shall not be placed in the District until all involuntary transfer teachers in that subject area have been placed.

(9) Every effort will be made to apply the principles of involuntary transfer to magnet schools and new schools; however, due to the special circumstances of these schools, final decisions shall be made on the basis of instructional requirements and students needs as determined by the Superintendent.

(10) The parties to this Agreement are committed to the goal of improving racial balance in the staffing of the schools of the District. Every reasonable effort will be made through hiring and attrition to improve the racial balance prior to any involuntary transfers.

10.04-REDUCTION IN FORCE: In the event that a reduction in force becomes necessary due to declines in enrollment, budgetary restrictions, reorganization, or other causes as determined by the Board, the following provisions shall apply.

10.041: The Board shall determine the specific work locations and/or special programs and areas of certification within which positions are to be eliminated. Once the specific areas of certification and/or positions have been determined, reductions shall be made on a districtwide basis and shall be based upon districtwide seniority and certification as further defined in this section.

10.042: For the purpose of reduction in force at the elementary level there shall be considered to be two areas of certification; kindergarten (to include early childhood certification) and elementary (grades 1–5).

10.043: In the middle and high schools, areas of certification shall be deemed to be the areas for which the employee holds certification and in which the employee has worked at least one (1) year within the past five (5) years.

10.044: In Special Education, consideration will be given to experience in working with the profoundly or the moderately handicapped.

10.045: Once specific positions and/or areas of certifications and levels have been identified by the Board, reduction in force shall be made on a districtwide basis as follows:

(1) Employees holding temporary and/or provisional certification will be the first reduced.

(2) Probationary employees who hold a professional teaching certificate will be the next reduced.

(3) Tenure employees will be the last reduced.

(4) With each of items sub 1–3, reduction shall be made such that persons in those areas having the least seniority will be the first released. Further reductions at each level shall be ascending order of seniority.

(5) Any employee whose job is to be eliminated by districtwide reduction in force shall be notified of such by certified mail.

(6) Before any reduction in force takes place, the Association shall be provided with a districtwide seniority list of all employees and the notification, the areas of certification, levels, work sites, and positions to be reduced.

(7) Once reduction in force has taken place on a districtwide basis, the appropriate reorganization of all available positions within all work sites shall be implemented according to any appropriate provisions in this Agreement and School Board policy. In every case where reorganization must take place, current employees shall be given the opportunity to volunteer to transfer prior to any involuntary transfer taking place.

10.06: TENTATIVE ASSIGNMENT AND CHANGES IN TENTATIVE ASSIGNMENTS: Each teacher shall be given a tentative teaching assignment in writing for the next school year prior to the last day of duty for the current year. This shall consist of the school and grade level for elementary; school, grade level and department for middle school; and school and department for high school to which the teacher is assigned. Every effort will be made to include course code number(s) and course title(s) for middle and high school teachers. In any event, middle and high school teachers will be notified in writing as soon as possible and not later than August 1 of their assignment by course number(s) and course title(s). Any teacher who desires a change in grade level and/or subject assignment shall file a written statement of this desire with the principal. No changes in the tentative assignment shall be made without attempts to arrange a prior conference with the teacher to provide rationale for the change and to address concerns of the teacher regarding the change. If a conference is not possible, the rationale for the change shall be submitted in writing to the teacher as soon as practicable prior to implementation of the change.

10.07-ADVERTISING AND FILLING VACANCIES: Teacher vacancies will be published weekly by the Human Resources Department during the regular school year. A vacancy shall exist when a person is sought to fill a full-time position which has been identified by the Human Resources Department. The notice of vacancies shall list the position, location, and qualifications including certification coverage for those positions, and deadline date for application. The notice of vacancies shall be sent to the Association. During the summer, teachers may dial the appropriate School Board number which provides a tape-recorded listing of current instructional vacancies.

10.072-Summer School: A list of anticipated summer school teaching vacancies and instructions for submitting applications shall be published in the District newsletter by May 1 of each year. Each assignment to a summer school position is tentative and subject to student attendance sufficient to warrant the position. Applicants shall be notified of tentative assignments by June 1. Applications of tenure teachers who have the appropriate certification and who are assigned during the regular school year to the schools, from which the summer school students are drawn, will be given first consideration.

10.075-Administrative Position Opportunities: Opportunities for Administrative positions shall be published at least twice annually in the notice of vacancies. During the summer opportunities for administrative positions will be available via telephone recording.

10.076-Filling Positions: Any applicant for an advertised vacancy received by the Human Resources Department from a district teacher shall be reviewed by the appropriate principal or supervisor prior to recommending an applicant to fill the position. Except in such circumstance as approved by the Superintendent, a vacancy will not be filled with other than an interim appointee for at least five (5) working days after the publishing date of the District newsletter listing the vacancy. Any tenure teacher holding the appropriate certification shall be given first consideration in the staffing of teaching vacancies. Teacher applicants in the District assigned to a grade level or subject area outside the scope of their teaching certification shall be given first consideration for openings within the subject or field of their certification.

ARTICLE 11
TEACHER ASSESSMENT

11.01: Within the first sixty (60) days of the teacher's contract year and prior to preparing the formal written report of a teacher assessment required by law, each teacher shall be informed of the criteria and procedures to be used in his/her formal observations and assessment.

11.012: Each teacher shall be the subject of a formal observation by the appropriate administrator at least two (2) times each school year. Employees who have tenure may elect an alternate assessment procedure in lieu of the formal observations subject to approval by the supervisor. Such procedures are outlined in the Board-approved District Performance Assessment Development System. Every reasonable effort will be made to ensure that the administrator is trained in the related performance measurement system. The first formal observation shall be completed by December 1. At least one formal observation of each classroom teacher is to be conducted by the principal or assistant principal. Other members of the instructional unit, including but not limited to, guidance counselors, media specialists, school social workers and school psychologists will be observed by an appropriate administrator.

11.013: All formal observations shall be reduced to writing and shall be discussed with the teacher prior to preparation of the teacher's assessment form. The teacher shall receive a copy of the formal observation report after signing to indicate that the report has been discussed with the teacher. If deficiencies are noted during the observation, the administrator conducting the observation shall provide the teacher with recommendations for improvement. The administrator shall thereafter confer with the teacher and make recommendations as to specific areas of unsatisfactory performance and provide assistance in helping to correct such deficiencies within a prescribed period of time.

11.014: Observations of a teacher's performance of duties and responsibilities shall be conducted openly with no intent to conceal such from the knowledge of the teacher.

11.015: Each teacher's formal written report of assessment shall be discussed with him/her by the administrator responsible for preparing the report.

11.016: After discussion of the assessment report with each teacher, the teacher shall sign the report, acknowledging that he/she has been shown the report, and it has been discussed with him/her by the assessor.

11.017: If a teacher disagrees with the formal written report of assessment, he/she may submit a written statement which shall, upon request of the teacher, be attached to the Board's file copy of his/her assessment report.

11.018: All probationary teachers shall be notified of their reappointment decision by the principal/supervisor by May 1.

11.019: The date for completion of a probationary teacher's formal written assessment shall be May 1. The date for completion of a tenured teacher's formal written assessment shall be May 1. These assessments may be performed earlier when notice of dismissal or nonrenewal is given.

11.022-COLLEGIAL COACH: Upon receipt of written notice of unsatisfactory evaluation from the Superintendent during the school year, a tenure teacher may select a collegial coach for the purpose of providing professional support and feedback. The individual designated as the collegial coach shall be decided upon mutual agreement among the principal, teacher, and collegial coach. The collegial coach will not participate in the formal evaluation of the teacher. The teacher may request an opportunity to be considered for a transfer to another school upon written request to the Superintendent.

ARTICLE 12
PROVISIONS FOR LEAVES

12.02-TYPES OF LEAVE:

12.0201-Sick Leave: Any teacher on a full-time basis shall be entitled to four (4) days of sick leave as of the first day of employment during each contract year and thereafter shall accrue one (1) day of sick leave credit for each month of employment. Sick leave shall be credited to the teacher at the end of the month and may not be used prior to the time it is earned and credited, provided that no teacher may earn more than one (1) day of sick leave times the number of months of employment during the school year. Such leave shall be cumulative (actual number of hours earned) from year to year without limit to the number of hours that may be accrued. Any leave charged against accrued sick leave shall be with full compensation. As stated above, the teacher receives four (4) sick days at the end of the first day of the contract year, but does not actually earn those four (4) days until he/she has worked four (4) months of the contract year. Therefore, if termination occurs when the employee has used more sick days than he/she has earned that contract year, and if he/she has no sick leave accumulated from prior years, the School Board will withhold the amount of the teacher's daily rate of pay for each sick day used that hasn't been earned. Also, if an employee who is eligible for terminal sick pay benefits terminates before completion of his/her contract year, the number of sick leave days for which he/she receives benefit shall not exceed the number of sick leave days accumulated prior to the beginning of that contact year plus one (1) sick leave day for each month of actual employment in the contract year during which termination occurs.

(1) **Claims:** Sick leave claims may be submitted by the teacher for his/her own personal illness as well as illness or death of father, mother, brother, sister, husband, wife, child or other close relative, or member of his/her own household.

(4) **Application for Sick Leave:** Teachers shall notify the appropriate administrator, with as much advance notice as possible, when the use of sick leave is necessary. A claim for sick leave on the proper form shall be signed by the teacher and filed with the principal or other immediate supervisor by the end of the fifth (5th) working day following the employee's return to work.

(5) **Conditions for Sick Leave:**

   b. Any teacher who has used all accrued sick leave but who is otherwise entitled to sick leave shall be granted sick leave without pay. The claim for such sick leave shall clearly state that the leave is without compensation.

   e. An application for sick leave due to an extended illness (not fewer than twenty [20] days) shall have attached to it a statement from a practicing physician certifying that such a leave is essential and indicating the probable duration of the illness and needed leave.

12.0203-Personal Leave:

(3) **Personal Leave (Without Pay):** Personal leave without pay will not be approved except in those instances where the teacher has no appropriate paid leave available. It is understood that a teacher's willingness to undertake leave without pay does not impose a requirement on the principal or the supervisor to approve the request for leave. The request is subject to approval or disapproval by the Superintendent based on the extent to which the teacher's absence will impact the instructional setting or the work setting.

a. **Extended Personal Leave (Without Pay)**: Personal leave without pay not to exceed thirty (30) days may be granted at the discretion of the Superintendent. Personal leave in excess of thirty (30) days shall be subject to approval by the Board.

ARTICLE 16
COMPENSATION

16.01-SALARIES: Each teacher shall be paid in accordance with the yearly salary schedule. The parties agree there shall be step progression for all eligible teachers on the salary schedule for the life of this contract.

16.012: Teachers who, during the 196–day work year, are employed for instruction beyond the defined teacher workday will be paid according to their current hourly rate, exclusive of any supplements paid.

16.013: Teacher participation in voluntary workshops or in-service training outside the school year may be paid a stipend determined by the School Board.

16.014: A maximum of ten (10) years' experience in out-of-state public schools, state colleges and universities, US government schools for dependents, public school in the American Virgin Islands, Guam, American Samoan Islands, and Puerto Rico shall be allowed for salary credit. A maximum of twelve (12) years' experience in other public school districts within the state shall be allowed for salary credit. To be eligible, creditable experience must have been attained after the person held a valid teaching certificate and a 4–year degree except when specified otherwise by State certification rules.

ARTICLE 18
ALCOHOL- AND DRUG-FREE WORKPLACE

18.01: No employee shall possess, consume or sell alcoholic beverages or manufacture, distribute, dispense, possess or use, on the job or in the workplace any narcotic, drug, amphetamine, barbiturate, marijuana, or any other controlled substance, as defined in the Controlled Substances Act.

18.02: "Workplace" is defined as the site for the performance of work done in connection with the duties of an employee of the Melita Public Schools. That term includes any place where the work of the School District is performed, including a building or other school premises; any school-owned vehicle or any other school-approved vehicle used to transport students to and from school or school activities; and off-school property during any school-sponsored or school-approved activity, event or function (such as a field trip, workshop, or athletic event). The workplace does not include duty-free time at conventions or workshops at which students are not present.

18.05: No employee shall be required to submit to drug or alcohol testing without reasonable suspicion except as otherwise required by law or this agreement. All drug and alcohol testing shall be conducted in accordance with District policy and procedures for drug and alcohol testing.

18.06: Possession of use of prescription drugs by an employee for which he/she hold the prescription is exempt from this section.

ARTICLE 19
MISCELLANEOUS

19.03: Should any article, section or clause of this Agreement be declared illegal by a court of competent jurisdiction or as a result of state or federal legislation which validly affects such article, section or clause, the parties shall meet to modify such article, section or clause to the extent necessary to bring it into legal compliance. The remaining articles, sections and clauses shall remain in full force and effect for the duration of the Agreement.

Appendix B

Selected[1] Contract Language
from the Agreement between the
Board of Education of the Melita Public Schools
and the
Melita Support Staff Association

ARTICLE 5
GRIEVANCE PROCEDURE

5.01-DEFINITION: A grievance is defined as a claim by a named employee, or a group of named employees, or the Association through the President, that there has been a violation, misinterpretation or misapplication of articles in this Agreement. A grievance shall be processed as hereinafter provided.

5.07-GRIEVANCE PROCEDURES:

STEP I: A copy of the grievance shall be forwarded by the grievant to the Superintendent and to the Association at the same time the grievance is filed with the supervisor. The supervisor shall meet with the grievant and his representative(s). Such meeting shall require at least two (2) working days' notice and shall be held within ten (10) working days of the date of filing the formal grievance. The supervisor shall furnish his written disposition of the grievance to the grievant within seven (7) working days of the meeting and shall furnish a copy thereof to the grievant, Superintendent, and the Association.

STEP II: If the grievant is not satisfied with the disposition of the grievance, or if no disposition has been made within the time limits as specified in Step I, the grievant may submit the same grievance to the Superintendent within ten (10) working days of the date of the disposition or the expiration of the time limits for a disposition. The Superintendent shall meet with the grievant and his representative(s) within ten (10) working days of the date of filing. The Superintendent shall furnish his written disposition of the grievance to the grievant within seven (7)

---

[1]This appendix includes only selected contract language. The language provided herein is that which is considered necessary background information for those working through the exercises included in chapter 4 of this publication.

working days of such meeting and shall furnish a copy thereof to the supervisor and to the Association.

STEP III: In the event the grievant is not satisfied with the disposition of the grievance at Step II, or if no disposition has been made within the time limits as provided in Step II, the grievant, with approval from and representation by the Association, may submit the grievance to arbitration in accordance with the rules of the American Arbitration Association. Submission of a grievance to arbitration shall be initiated by the grievant, his counsel or by his designated Association representative, by filing a written request with the American Arbitration Association and the Superintendent within ten (10) working days of the date of the Step II disposition of the grievance or the expiration of time limits for a disposition. The disposition of the grievance made by the arbitrator shall be binding on both parties, providing that the arbitrator shall have no power to add to, subtract from, modify, or otherwise alter the terms of the collective bargaining agreement. The grievance may be settled while the arbitration procedure is pending.

5.08-EXPENSES: The fees and expenses of the arbitrator and witness fees for witnesses called by the arbitrator shall be paid equally by the Board and the Association. Otherwise, each party shall bear its own expenses.

ARTICLE 6
EMPLOYEE WORKING CONDITIONS

6.021-CHANGES IN ALLOCATIONS: When allocations at any work site require that any employee have a change in hours, the employee shall be notified of the change five (5) days prior to the effective date of the change, except for the first fifteen (15) days of the school year. Employees shall be reduced in hours due to changes in work site allocations in order of their District seniority, from least seniority to greatest seniority provided the senior employee has the ability to perform the available work in a satisfactory manner. Employees shall be increased in hours due to changes in work site allocations in descending District seniority provided the senior employee has the ability to perform the available work in a satisfactory manner.

6.03-OVERTIME: All authorized work performed in excess of forty (40) hours in any one week shall be considered overtime and shall be paid at the overtime rate of one and one–half (1½) times the employee's regular rate of pay. Paid holidays and sick leave for one day during the work week shall be counted and time worked for the purpose of computing overtime.

6.04-REST PERIODS: Employees who work six (6) continuous hours per day or more shall receive two (2) rest periods of fifteen (15) minutes each, preferably one in the morning and one in the afternoon except as follows:

6.042: Employees who work four (4) or more, but less than six (6), continuous hours will receive at least one fifteen (15) minute rest period per day.

ARTICLE 7
GENERAL EMPLOYMENT PRACTICES

7.02-VOLUNTARY TRANSFER TO ANOTHER SCHOOL OR SITE

7.021: Each employee may request a transfer by contacting the supervisor or principal at the site in which a vacancy exists and request an interview. When two (2) or more employees apply for the same position, the employee with the most in-district seniority will be given first consideration.

7.03-INVOLUNTARY TRANSFER TO ANOTHER SCHOOL OR SITE

7.031: The Board shall determine the criteria for the selection of employees to be involuntarily transferred. Such criteria shall be applied uniformly throughout the District. An employee selected for an involuntary transfer shall be given the reason for such transfer and the opportunity to object to his supervisor about such transfer. If requested by the employee, the reason shall be given in writing.

7.032: Transfers shall be made on a voluntary basis, whenever possible; however, correct and proper operation of the School District will necessarily require that involuntary transfers be made.

7.033: Prior to determining involuntary transfers, employees shall be given an opportunity to volunteer.

7.034: Involuntary transfers may be made in the event of a school closing.

7.035: Involuntary transfers may be made to achieve a reduction in the number of employees assigned to a school. Subject to job requirements and students' needs, employees selected for involuntary transfers shall be those with the least District seniority.

7.036: A list of employees to be involuntarily transferred will be compiled by the Human Resources Department. Vacancy information shall be provided to these employees. Thereafter, employees shall indicate the positions, in order of preference, which they desire. After consideration of job requirements and student needs, employees who have the highest seniority shall be placed first.

7.037: No new employee shall be hired in a job classification until all employees in that classification have been placed. Should an employee refuse to accept an assignment substantially equal to the current assignment, said refusal shall constitute a resignation by the employee.

7.06-SENIORITY AND REDUCTION-IN-FORCE

7.062-Layoff: The Board will determine the classification by departments and schools to be reduced. The Board will notify the Association in advance of any reduction-in-force or reduction in hours action. Employees will be laid off or reduced in hours in the inverse order of their seniority in the District. Employees who are laid off or reduced in hours may fill a vacant position, if qualified.

7.07-EMPLOYEE PERFORMANCE ASSESSMENT: Each employee will receive a written performance assessment of his work at least once during each contract year.

7.071: Each employee's written performance assessment shall be discussed with him by the supervisor.

7.072: After discussion of the performance assessment, the employee shall sign the performance assessment, acknowledging that he has been shown the report and that it has been discussed with him by the assessor.

7.073: If the employee disagrees with his performance assessment, he may submit a written statement which shall, upon request of the employee, be attached to the Board's copy.

7.074: Each employee shall be given a copy of his performance assessment within ten (10) calendar days after completion; but not later than April 1. Additional performance assessments completed after April 1 will be given to each employee within ten (10) calendar days after completion.

7.075: All discussion of a performance assessment by a supervisor shall be conducted in private.

7.076: No employee in the unit shall complete or sign performance assessments of other employees.

7.09-DISCIPLINE: Allegations of employee misconduct or unsatisfactory job performance shall be reviewed by the Director of Human Resources at the request of the employee's supervisor. The Department of Human Resources shall conduct an informal predetermination conference to review the allegations. Employees will be given at least two (2) days' prior written notice, whenever possible, of the predetermination conference and shall be advised of their right to have a representative accompany them and present relevant information. After all information has been considered, the Director of Human Resources shall make a recommendation of any disciplinary action to the Superintendent. Recommended action may include, but are not limited to, letters of warning and reprimand, suspension without pay, retraining or other assistance and dismissal from employment.

7.091-Reprimand: Any written reprimand (or warning) shall be furnished to the employee and the employee shall sign the reprimand or warning for the sole purpose of indicating that he has received the statement and has discussed it with the supervisor. If the employee refuses to sign, the reprimand will be provided to the employee and placed in the employee's personnel file. The employee will have an opportunity to submit a written response which will be placed in the employee's personnel file.

7.092-Suspension: Suspensions shall be subject to the grievance procedure. In the event that grievant prevails, the suspension shall be removed from all personnel files. All notices of suspension shall be in writing and delivered to the employee with a copy to the Association within five (5) days of the decision to suspend.

7.093-Dismissal: The employee and the Association shall receive written notice of a recommendation for dismissal. Such notice shall include the reasons for the recommendation to dismiss. The employee shall either be entitled to a hearing before the Board or may file a grievance but may not do both.

7.094: Any discipline during the contract year, that constitutes a reprimand, suspension, demotion or termination shall be for just cause.

7.10-NONREAPPOINTMENT: During the first three (3) years of employment and upon written request, the employee shall be granted a conference with the Superintendent for the purposes of reviewing the Supervisor's recommendation not to renew the employee's contract. The employee must request the conference within five (5) workdays after receiving notification from his/her supervisor that nonrenewal is being recommended. The Superintendent shall conduct the conference within ten (10) working days of the employee's request. The decision of the Superintendent shall be in writing and shall be furnished to the employee within ten (10) work days after the conference. The decision is final and not subject to the grievance procedure unless it is arbitrary or capricious. After three (3) years of successful employment, no employee's contract shall be nonrenewed except for just cause.

7.101: An employee who is being considered for nonreappointment due to poor performance shall receive written notice from the supervisor by May 1.

7.102: An employee who is being considered for nonreappointment based upon misconduct occurring after May 1 will receive written notice as soon as that decision is made by the supervisor.

ARTICLE 8
JOB POSTING, BIDDING AND PROMOTIONS

8.01: Job openings and new positions shall be filled as herein provided.

8.011: When job vacancies occur, the applicant whose qualifications, work experience and interview responses are superior, shall be offered the position. Any job specific skills, knowledge, abilities and qualification in addition to the approved job description expected of applicants shall be determined prior to considering any applicants for a vacancy. Additional skills, knowledge, abilities and qualification shall not be to the extent that it would create a new job classification or be equivalent to an existing job classification and job description. Current employees of the District who apply shall be given first consideration prior to other applicants. If the Superintendent determines that two or more current employee applicants are equally qualified, the employee applicant with the most in-district experience will be offered the position. If an unsuccessful employee applicant makes a written request to the supervisor responsible for the selection process within ten (10) working days of his interview appointment, the supervisor will schedule a conference within ten (10) days of receipt of the written request to discuss his application and possible changes to enhance the employee's opportunity for future promotion.

196

8.05-SUBSTITUTES: If an employee is on an approved leave of absence, and no substitute is utilized, no additional duties shall be distributed to other employees unless comparable duties are specified by the principal, supervisor or designee as duties not to be completed.

8.08-SUBCONTRACTING: The Board agrees to utilize subcontractors only for a specific need or in case of an emergency.

ARTICLE 9
LEAVES

9.026-JURY DUTY LEAVE: Any employee, including those employed for summer school, who is subpoenaed for jury duty shall be granted temporary duty leave with pay. The employee shall not be reimbursed for meals, lodging and travel while on leave. Per diem paid by the court for such purposes may be retained by the employee.

9.029-MEDICAL LEAVE:
    11.**Fitness-for-Duty Certification:** As a condition of restoration of an employee who has taken medical leave due to the employee's serious health condition, the employee is required to provide certification from the employee's health care provider that the employee is able to resume work, i.e., is fit for duty.

ARTICLE 11
MISCELLANEOUS

11.04-CRIMINAL CONVICTIONS: Each employee shall be responsible for notifying his/her immediate supervisor, as soon as he/she becomes aware of any conviction on a misdemeanor or felony charge involving moral turpitude. Unit employees who regularly or incidentally operate Board vehicles shall, as soon as they become aware, notify their supervisor of any moving violation, suspension or revocation of their driver's license. Failure to comply with any provision of this section may be cause for appropriate disciplinary action. Such disciplinary action shall be subject to the grievance procedure.

ARTICLE 16
ALCOHOL- AND DRUG-FREE WORKPLACE

16.01: No employee shall possess, consume or sell alcoholic beverages or manufacture, distribute, dispense, possess or use, on the job or in the workplace, any narcotic drug, amphetamine, barbiturate, marijuana, or other controlled substance, as defined in the Controlled Substances Act.

16.05: No employee shall be required to submit to drug or alcohol testing without reasonable suspicion except as otherwise required by law or this agreement. All drug and alcohol testing shall be conducted in accordance with District policy and procedures for drug and alcohol testing.

16.06: Possession or use of prescription drugs by an employee for which he holds the prescription is exempt from this section.

Subject Index

ABOUT THE AUTHORS

Jerry R. Baker received his bachelor's degree from Central Michigan University in 1960 and his master's in Educational Administration from this same university in 1963. In 1977, he received his Ph.D. from The Ohio State University. His career in education has spanned more than four decades. He has worked in three Michigan K–12 school districts and one in Florida, serving as a teacher, counselor, director of research and evaluation, and for 20 years as an assistant superintendent for human resources. His last K–12 district provided services to 54,000 students and employed 7,000 full-time employees. Currently he is a Professor of Educational Leadership at Saginaw Valley State University (SVSU). At SVSU he teaches courses in human resource management and educational administration. Additionally, he serves on the advisory board of the university's Office of Equal Opportunity. He maintains contact with public school districts through his consulting work that primarily involves improving practice in human resource management and conducting research/evaluation at the district level. For his work in the area of research/evaluation, he has been given the Phi Delta Kappa (PDK) "Leadership in Research Award."

Madeleine S. Doran, originally from Valdosta, Georgia, has a bachelor's degree in Business Education from Valdosta State University, a master's in Business Administration from the University of Montana and an Ed.D. from the University of South Florida in Educational Administration. She is listed in the 1970 edition of the Outstanding Young Women of America. Doran held increasingly responsible positions in public schools serving as a teacher, systems analyst, consultant, assistant director and director of personnel and school board labor negotiator. Her 15 years of experience in human resources, including labor negotiations, was obtained while working for one of the 100 largest school districts in the United States. She has presented a number of workshops on employment issues and has authored articles of interest to human resource practitioners. Doran is also active in numerous civic and charitable activities, ranging from animal rights organizations to local government commissions. She is presently Associate Professor in Barry University's graduate Human Resource Development program and teaches courses in Theory and Practice in Human Resources, Legal Issues in Human Resources and Adult Motivation and Organizational Learning.